Moodle

E-Learning Course Development

A complete guide to successful learning using

William H. Rice IV

[PACKT]
PUBLISHING

BIRMINGHAM - MUMBAI

Moodle

E-Learning Course Development

First published: May 2006

Production Reference: 1160506

Published by Packt Publishing Ltd.
32 Lincoln Road
Olton
Birmingham, B27 6PA, UK.

ISBN 1-904811-29-9

www.packtpub.com

Cover Design by www.visionwt.com

Credits

Author
William H. Rice IV

Reviewers
Mark Bailye
Gurudutt Talgery

Technical Editor
Heidi Pearl

Editorial Manager
Dipali Chittar

Development Editor
David Barnes

Indexer
Abhishek Shirodkar

Proofreader
Chris Smith

Production Coordinator
Manjiri Nadkarni

Cover Designer
Helen Wood

About the Author

William H. Rice IV is a training manager, a technical writer, and a knowledge manager who lives and works in New York City. He has been helping people to incorporate technology into their work processes since graduating with a degree in technical writing in 1988. He has developed training and documentation for Fortune 100 clients, hospitals, small businesses, and universities. His first book for Packt Publishing was *User Training for Busy Programmers*, ISBN 1-904811-45-0.

When William isn't working, he enjoys foraging for edible wild plants in New York City parks, hiking and climbing in Pennsylvania, and archery within sight of J.F.K. International Airport. His current favorite blog is www.43folders.com. His favorite non-work activity is spending time with his beautiful wife and child.

William maintains an online magazine for technical trainers and writers at www.williamrice.com. On this website, other trainers and writers are welcome to browse and submit articles. He can be reached through his website or at techcomm@williamrice.com.

For my father, William III, who instilled in me a curiosity and love of learning; and for William V, to whom I hope to pass on this wonderful legacy.

About the Reviewers

Gurudutt Talgery has close to twenty years of industry experience in areas of software development, software process, and product engineering working in the Indian arms of such companies as Texas Instruments and Tektronix. His area of interest is Digital Asset Management and Search Applications using open source solution stacks. He believes that technology exists for people rather than the other way round. When not thinking about asset management and search interfaces, Gurudutt dabbles into Oriental philosophy, Indic computing, and living a cyberlife exclusively on open source technologies. Gurudutt lives in Bangalore, India with his family.

Table of Contents

Preface

This book shows you how to use Moodle as a tool to enhance your teaching. Initially, it will help you to analyze your students' requirements, and understand what Moodle can do for them. After that you'll see how to use different features of Moodle to meet your course goals.

The social constructionist learning philosophy is at the heart of Moodle: we all *construct* knowledge through interaction with one another and with learning materials in a social way. This book will show you how to add static learning material, interactive activities, and social features to your courses so that students reach their learning potential.

Whether you want to support traditional class teaching or lecturing, or provide complete online and distance learning courses, this book will prove a powerful resource throughout your use of Moodle.

What You Need for This Book

- Access to a server capable of running Moodle, or a server with Moodle installed already.
- A computer with Internet access.
- Instructor or administrator access to Moodle, if it's installed already.
- A fairly new web browser (anything less than 18 months old should be fine).

Who is This Book For?

This book is for anyone who wants to make the most of Moodle's features to produce an interactive online learning experience. If you're an educator, corporate trainer, or just someone with something to teach, this book can guide you through the installation, configuration, creation, and management of a Moodle site. It is suitable for people who perform the task of creating and setting up the learning site, and for those who create and deliver courses on the site. That is, it is for site administrators, course creators, and teachers.

Conventions

In this book, you will find a number of styles of text that distinguish between different kinds of information. Here are some examples of these styles, and an explanation of their meaning.

There are three styles for code. Code words in text are shown as follows: "We can include other contexts through the use of the include directive."

A block of code will be set as follows:

```
<form name="redirect">
<center>
<font face="Arial"><b>You will be redirected to the script in<br><br>
<form>
<input type="text" size="3" name="redirect2">
```

When we wish to draw your attention to a particular part of a code block, the relevant lines or items will be made bold:

```
<form name="redirect">
<center>
<font face="Arial"><b>You will be redirected to the script in<br><br>
<form>
<input type="text" size="3" name="redirect2">
```

New terms and **important words** are introduced in a bold-type font. Words that you see on the screen, in menus or dialog boxes for example, appear in our text like this: "clicking the Next button moves you to the next screen".

Warnings or important notes appear in a box like this.

Reader Feedback

Feedback from our readers is always welcome. Let us know what you think about this book, what you liked or may have disliked. Reader feedback is important for us to develop titles that you really get the most out of.

To send us general feedback, simply drop an email to feedback@packtpub.com, making sure to mention the book title in the subject of your message.

If there is a book that you need and would like to see us publish, please send us a note in the SUGGEST A TITLE form on www.packtpub.com or email suggest@packtpub.com.

If there is a topic that you have expertise in and you are interested in either writing or contributing to a book, see our author guide on www.packtpub.com/authors.

Customer Support

Now that you are the proud owner of a Packt book, we have a number of things to help you to get the most from your purchase.

Errata

Although we have taken every care to ensure the accuracy of our contents, mistakes do happen. If you find a mistake in one of our books—maybe a mistake in text or code—we would be grateful if you would report this to us. By doing this you can save other readers from frustration, and help to improve subsequent versions of this book. If you find any errata, report them by visiting http://www.packtpub.com/support, selecting your book, clicking on the Submit Errata link, and entering the details of your errata. Once your errata have been verified, your submission will be accepted and the errata added to the list of existing errata. The existing errata can be viewed by selecting your title from http://www.packtpub.com/support.

Questions

You can contact us at questions@packtpub.com if you are having a problem with some aspect of the book, and we will do our best to address it.

1

Introduction

Moodle is a free learning management system that enables you to create powerful, flexible, and engaging online learning experiences. I use the phrase "online learning experiences" instead of "online courses" deliberately. The phrase "online course" often connotes a sequential series of web pages, some images, maybe a few animations, and a quiz put online. There might be some email or bulletin board communication between the teacher and students. However, online learning can be much more engaging than that.

Moodle's name gives you insight into its approach to e-learning. From the official Moodle documentation:

> The word Moodle was originally an acronym for **Modular Object-Oriented Dynamic Learning Environment**, which is mostly useful to programmers and education theorists. It's also a verb that describes the process of lazily meandering through something, doing things as it occurs to you to do them, an enjoyable tinkering that often leads to insight and creativity. As such it applies both to the way Moodle was developed, and to the way a student or teacher might approach studying or teaching an online course. Anyone who uses Moodle is a **Moodler**.

The phrase "online learning experience" connotes a more active, engaging role for the students and teachers. It connotes web pages that can be explored in any order, courses with live chats among students and teachers, forums where users can rate messages on their relevance or insight, online workshops that enable students to collaborate and evaluate each other's work, impromptu polls that let the teacher evaluate what students think of a course's progress, directories set aside for students to upload and share their files. All of these features create an active learning environment, full of different kinds of student-to-student and student-to-teacher interaction. This is the kind of user experience that Moodle excels at, and the kind that this book will help you to create.

A Plan for Creating Your Learning Site

Whether you are the site creator or a course creator, you can use this book as you would a project plan. As you work your way through each chapter, the book provides guidance on making decisions that meet your goals for your learning site. This helps you to create the kind of learning experience you want for your teachers (if you're the site creator) or students (if you're the teacher). You can also use this book as a traditional reference manual, but its main advantages are its step-by-step, project-oriented approach and the guidance it gives you about creating an interactive learning experience.

Moodle is designed to be intuitive to use and its online help is well written. It does a good job of telling you how to use each of its features. What Moodle's help files don't tell you is when and why to use each feature, and what effect it will have on the student experience; and that is what this book supplies.

The appendix contains a checklist of the major steps for creating a Moodle site and populating it with courses. The steps are cross-referenced to the relevant sections of this book. Download this checklist from the Packt Publishing website (http://www.packtpub.com), print it, and keep it handy while creating your Moodle site.

Step-By-Step: Using Each Chapter

When you create a Moodle learning site, you usually follow a defined series of steps. This book is arranged to support that process. Each chapter shows you how to get the most from each step. Each step is listed below, with a brief description of the chapter that supports the step.

As you work your way through each chapter, your learning site will grow in scope and sophistication. By the time you finish this book, you should have a complete, interactive learning site. As you learn more about what Moodle can do, and see your courses taking shape, you may want to change some things you did in previous chapters. Moodle offers you this flexibility. And, this book helps you determine how those changes will cascade throughout your site.

Step 1: Learn About the Moodle Experience (Chapter 1)

Every Learning Management System (LMS) has a paradigm, or approach, that shapes the user experience and encourages a certain kind of usage. An LMS might encourage very sequential learning by offering features that enforce a given order on each course. It might discourage student-to-student interaction by offering few features that support it, while encouraging solo learning by offering many opportunities for the student to interact with the course material. In this chapter, you will learn what Moodle can do and what kind of user experience your students and teachers will have, using Moodle. You will also learn about the Moodle philosophy, and how it shapes the user experience. With this information, you'll be ready to decide how to make the best use of Moodle's many features, and to plan your online learning site.

Step 2: Install and Configure Moodle (Chapter 2)

Most of the decisions you make while installing and configuring Moodle will affect the user experience. Not just students and teachers, but also course creators and site administrators are affected by these decisions. While Moodle's online help does a good job of telling you how to install and configure the software, it doesn't tell you how the settings you choose affect the user experience. Chapter 2 covers the implications of these decisions, and helps you configure the site so that it behaves in the way you envision.

Step 3: Create the Framework for Your Learning Site (Chapter 3)

In Moodle, every course belongs to a category. Chapter 3 takes you through creating course categories, and then creating courses. Just as you chose site-wide settings during installation and configuration, you choose course-wide settings while creating each course. This chapter tells you the implications of the various course settings so that you can create the experience you want for each course. Finally, Chapter 3 takes you through the usage of the various blocks, each of which adds a well-defined function to the site or to the course. After creating the categories and courses, and deciding which blocks to use, you've created a framework for your site. Then you're ready to fill your courses with learning material, which you'll do in Steps 4 through 6.

Step 4: Add Basic Course Material (Chapter 4)

In most online courses, the core material consists of web pages that the students view. These pages can contain text, graphics, movies, sound files, games, exercises: anything that can appear on the World Wide Web can appear on a Moodle web page. Chapter 4 covers adding web pages to Moodle courses, plus other kinds of static course material: plain-text pages, links to other websites, labels, and directories of files. This chapter also helps you determine when to use each of these types of material.

Step 5: Make Your Courses Interactive (Chapter 5)

In this context, "interactive" means interaction between the student and teacher, or the student and an active web page. Student-to-student interaction is covered in the next step. Interactive course material includes surveys posed by the teacher, journals written by the student and read only by the teacher, and lessons that guide students through a defined path based upon their answers to review questions and quizzes. Chapter 5 tells you how to create these interactions, and how each of them affects the student and teacher experience. You'll need this information to help you manage Moodle's interactive features.

Step 6: Make Your Course Social (Chapter 6)

Social course material enables student-to-student interaction. Moodle enables you to add chats, forums, and **Wikis** to your courses. These types of interactions will be familiar to many students. You can also create glossaries that are site-wide and specific to a single course. Students can add to the glossaries. Finally, Moodle offers a powerful workshop tool, which enables students to view and evaluate each others work. Each of these interactions makes the course more interesting, but also more complicated for the teacher to manage. Chapter 6 helps you to make the best use of Moodle's social features. The result is a course that encourages students to contribute, share, and evaluate.

Step 7: Create a Welcome for New and Existing Students (Chapter 7)

Chapter 7 helps you create a public face for your Moodle site. You can show a Login Page or the Front Page of your site. The content and behavior of the login and Front Pages can be customized. You can choose to allow anonymous users, require students to be registered, or use a combination of guest and registered access. Each of these options affects the kind of welcome that new and existing students get, when they first see your site. Chapter 7 helps you determine which options to use, and to combine them to get the effect you desire.

Step 8: Use Teacher's Tools to Deliver and Administer Courses (Chapter 8)

Moodle offers several tools to help teachers administer and deliver courses. It keeps detailed access logs that enable teachers to see exactly what content students accessed, and when. It also enables teachers to establish custom grading scales, which are available site-wide or for a single course. Student grades can be accessed online and also downloaded to a spreadsheet program. Finally, teachers can collaborate in special forums (bulletin boards) reserved just for them.

Step 9: Extend Moodle (Chapter 9)

Because Moodle is open source, new modules are constantly being developed and contributed by the Moodle community. The modules that are part of Moodle's core distribution are covered in this book. Additional modules extend Moodle's capabilities. While this book cannot cover every module available, it can cover the process of installing and integrating new modules into your site. One of the modules included with the core distribution is a **PayPal** module. Chapter 9 covers using this module for pay sites. This chapter also covers backing up and restoring the entire site, individual courses, and components within a course.

The Moodle Philosophy

Moodle is designed to support a style of learning called *Social Constructionist Pedagogy*. This style of learning is interactive. The social constructionist philosophy believes that people learn best when they interact with the learning material, construct new material for others, and interact with other students about the material. The difference between a traditional class and the social constructionist philosophy is the difference between a lecture and a discussion.

Moodle does not require you to use the social constructionist method for your courses. However, it best supports this method. For example, Moodle enables you to add five kinds of static course material. This is course material that a student reads, but does not interact with:

- A text page
- A web page
- A link to anything on the Web (including material on your Moodle site)
- A view into one of the course's directories
- A label that displays any text or image

However, Moodle also enables you to add six types of interactive course material. This is course material that a student interacts with, by answering questions, entering text, or uploading files:

- Assignment (uploading files to be reviewed by the teacher and/or students)
- Choice (a single question)
- Journal (an online journal)
- Lesson (a conditional, branching activity)
- Quiz (an online test)
- Survey (with results available to the teacher and/or students)

Moodle also offers five kinds of activities where students interact with each other. These are used to create social course material:

- Chat (live online chat between students)
- Forum (you can choose the number of online bulletin boards for each course)
- Glossary (students and/or teachers can contribute terms to site-wide glossaries)
- Wiki (Wikis can be inserted into courses, or a Wiki can be the entire course)
- Workshop (workshops support collaborative, graded efforts among students)

That's five kinds of static course material, and eleven kinds of interactive course material. In addition, some of Moodle's add-on modules add even more types of interaction. For example, one add-on module enables students and teachers to schedule appointments with each other.

The Moodle Experience

Because Moodle encourages interaction and exploration, your students' learning experience will often be nonlinear. Conversely, Moodle has few features for enforcing a specific order upon a course. For example, there is no feature in Moodle that would require a student to complete Course 101 before allowing the student to enroll in Course 102. Instead, you would need to manually enroll the student in each course. Also, there is no Moodle feature that would require a student to complete Topic 1 in a course before allowing the student to see Topic 2. If you wanted to enforce that kind of linear course flow, you would need to manually place the student into the group that is authorized to view Topic 1, and then upon completion, place the student in to the group that is authorized to view Topics 1 and 2, and so on.

As a site administrator or teacher, enforcing a linear path through a course catalogue, or through the material in an individual course, often requires manual intervention. However, if you design your site with Moodle's nonlinear style in mind, you will find it offers you great flexibility and the ability to create engaging online courses.

In this section, I'll take you on a tour of a Moodle learning site. You will see the student's experience from the time the student arrives at the site, enters a course, and works through some material in the course. You will also see some student-to-student interaction, and some functions used by the teacher to manage the course. Along the way, I'll point out many of the features that you will learn to implement in this book, and how the demo site uses those features.

The Moodle Front Page

The Front Page of your site is the first thing most visitors will see. This section takes you on a tour of the Front Page of my demonstration site.

Arriving at the Site

When a potential student arrives at the demonstration learning site, the student sees the Front Page. Later in this book, you'll learn to control what an anonymous visitor to your learning site sees on the Front Page. You can even require the visitor to register and log in before seeing any part of your site. Like most sites, my demonstration site allows anonymous visitors to see a lot of information about the site:

One of the first things a visitor will notice is the announcement at the top and centre of the page, Desert Plants Course Added. Below the announcement are two activities: a quiz, Win a Prize: Test Your Wilderness Knowledge, and a chat room, Global Chat Room. Selecting either of these activities will require to the student to register with the site:

Anonymous, Guest, and Registered Access

Notice the line Some courses may allow guest access at the middle of the page. You can set three levels of access for your entire site, and for individual courses:

Anonymous access allows anyone to access the site or course.

Guest access requires the user to login as guest. This enables you to track usage, by looking at the statistics for the user guest. But since everyone is logged in as the user guest, you can't track individual users.

Registered access requires the user to register on your site. You can allow people to register with or without email confirmation, require a special code for enrolment, and/or manually create/confirm their accounts.

The Main Menu

Returning to the Front Page, notice the Main menu in the upper left corner. This menu consists of three documents that tell the user what the site is about, and how to use it.

In Moodle, icons tell the user what kind of resource will be accessed by a link. In this case, the icon tells the user these are web or text pages. Course materials that a student observes or reads, such as web or text pages, hyperlinks, and multimedia files are called **Resources**. In Chapter 4, you will learn how to add Resources to a course.

Blocks

Below the Main menu is a Calendar and the Upcoming Events. These are **Blocks**, which you can choose to add to the Front Page and to each course individually.

Other blocks display a summary of the current course, a list of courses available on the site, the latest news that is online, and other information. In the lower right of the Front Page you see the Login block. Chapter 3 tells you how to use these blocks.

You can add these blocks to the Front Page of your site because the Front Page is essentially a course. Anything that you can add to course—such as Resources and Blocks, can be added to the Front Page.

Site Description

On the right side of the Front Page you see a Site Description. This is optional. If this were a course, you could choose to display the Course Description.

Welcome to the *Wilderness Skills* site. If you have an interest in primitive living/survival skills, you're at the right place. This site offers courses in basic botany (just enough for a beginning forager), shelter building, firestarting without matches, orienteering, and other wilderness skills.

The Site or Course Description can contain anything that you can put on a web page. It is essentially a block of HTML code that is put onto the Front Page.

Available Courses

You can choose to display available courses on the Front Page of your site. In the Demonstration site, I've created a category for Free Courses and another for Wild Plants. Free courses allow anonymous users to enter. Courses in other categories require users to register.

Clicking on the information icon ❶ next to each course displays the Course Description. Clicking on a course name takes you into the course. If the course allows anonymous access, you are taken directly into the course. If the course allows guest access, or requires registration, you are taken to the Login screen.

Inside a Course

Now let us take a look inside the course.

Breadcrumbs

In the screenshot given previously, the user has logged in as guest and entered the Basic Botany course. We know this from the breadcrumb trail at the top left of the screen, which tells us the name of the site and of the course. In the upper right, we see a confirmation that the user has logged in under the name guest.

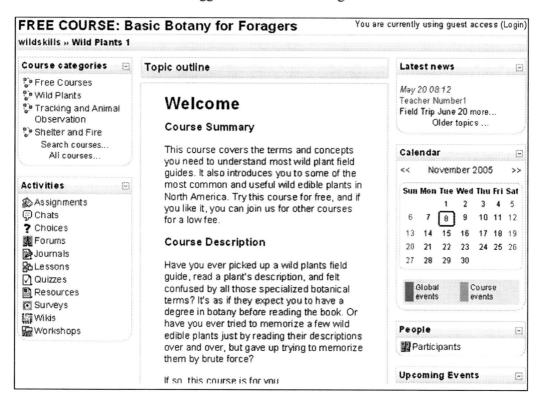

Blocks

Like the Front Page, this course displays the Calendar and Upcoming Events blocks. It also displays blocks for the Latest news, People, Activities, and Course categories. The Activities block lists all of the types of Activities and Resources that are in this course. Clicking on a link will display that type of activity. For example, clicking Quizzes displays this screen:

wildskills » Wild Plants 1 » Quizzes			
Topic	Name	Quiz closes	Best grade
2	Life Cycles of Plants	Thursday, November 9 2006, 04:50 AM	
3	Leaf Types and Shapes	Saturday, July 8 2006, 04:15 PM	

Notice the breadcrumbs at the top now indicate the site name, course name, and that you are viewing the quizzes in the course. The course is organized by Topic, and the number of each Topic is displayed in the left column. Because the user is logged in as guest, and many users can use that ID, the Best grade column is not meaningful here. It indicates only the highest grade for everyone who has ever attempted this quiz with guest access. Clicking on the name of a quiz takes the user to that quiz. Clicking on Wild Plants 1, takes the user back to the course.

Earlier, I commented on the nonlinear nature of most Moodle courses. Notice that even though the user has not completed Topic 1, the quizzes for Topic 2 and 3 are open to the user. Also, looking at the Activities block, you can see that all of the resources for this course are available to the user at all times.

Topics

Moodle also enables you to organize a course by Week, in which case each section is labeled with a date instead of a number. Or, you can choose to make your course a single, large discussion forum.

Topic outline

Welcome

Course Summary

This course covers the terms and concepts you need to understand most wild plant field guides. It also introduces you to some of the most common and useful wild edible plants in North America. Try this course for free, and if you like it, you can join us for other courses for a low fee.

Course Description

Have you ever picked up a wild plants field guide, read a plant's description, and felt confused by all those specialized botanical terms? It's as if they expect you to have a degree in botany before reading the book. Or have you ever tried to memorize a few wild edible plants just by reading their descriptions over and over, but gave up trying to memorize them by brute force?

If so, this course is for you.

Welcome to *Basic Botany for Foragers*. This course introduces you to foraging. Foraging is identifying, gathering, and using wild plants for food, medicine, and tools.

Before continuing, it is very important that you read and understand the following warning: **Eat only those plants you can positively identify and that you know are safe to eat. Identify and collect wild plants only under the guidance of an experienced forager. This course is an excellent preparation for learning to identify plants under the guidance of an expert, but is not a substitute. You should learn under someone qualified and experienced in the collection of wild plants in your area. Common sense dictates that if you have any doubt as to a plant's safety, don't eat it.**

To learn more about this course, select *Course Goals and Outline* below. To meet your fellow foragers, join the *Course Discussion*. To jump into the course, just select a lesson.

🔖 Course Goals and Outline
💬 Wild Plants Chat Room

Jump to a Topic

Types of Plants

Life Cycles of Plants

Leaves

Flowers

Roots

Other Identifying Features

Habitats

Group Activities

▓ Course Discussion
▓ Group Wiki

Before You Start the Course: Do These Activities

🐾 The Plants Around You
? Have you tried edible wild plants?
📑 Foraging Journal

---

1 ☐

Types of Plants

Identifying the basic types of plants: woody, herbaceous, and succulents.

🔖 Types of Plants
🎴 What kind of plant is it?

---

2 ☐

Life Cycles of Plants

Like all living things, plants have a life cycle. This lesson covers the different types of life cycles found in the plant world.

📄 Life Cycles of Plants

Most courses are organized by Topic. Notice that the first topic, which I've labeled Welcome, is not numbered. Moodle gives you a Topic 0 to use as the course introduction.

Course creators can hide and show topics at will. Teachers can be given course creator rights to a course, so that the teachers can also show/hide topics as the course progresses.

Topics are the lowest level of organization in Moodle. The hierarchy is Site | Course Category | Course Subcategory (optional) | Course | Topic. Every item in your course belongs to a Topic, even if your course consists of only Topic 0.

Join a Discussion

Clicking on Course Discussion, under Group Activities, takes the student to the course-wide forum. You can see in this screenshot that the teacher started with the first post. Then William Rice left a test message, and a student replied to the original post:

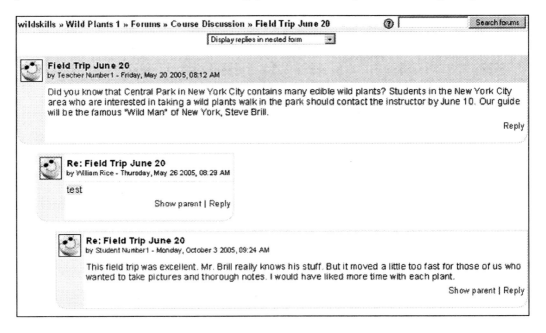

That test message doesn't serve our students. Fortunately, the teacher has editing rights to this forum, and so he or she can delete posts at will. The teacher can also rate posts for their relevance, as shown next:

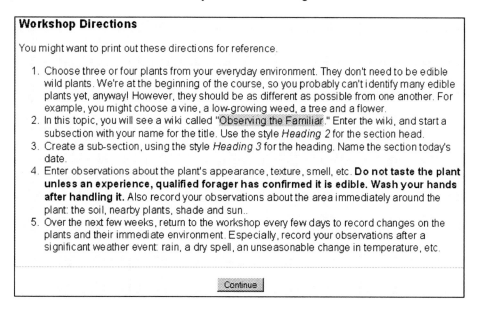

Because Moodle supports an interactive, collaborative style of learning, students can also be given the ability to rate forum posts and material submitted by other students. You'll find out more about forums in Chapter 6.

Complete a Workshop

Next, the student will enter a workshop called Observing the Familiar.

Workshop Directions

You might want to print out these directions for reference.

1. Choose three or four plants from your everyday environment. They don't need to be edible wild plants. We're at the beginning of the course, so you probably can't identify many edible plants yet, anyway! However, they should be as different as possible from one another. For example, you might choose a vine, a low-growing weed, a tree and a flower.
2. In this topic, you will see a wiki called "Observing the Familiar." Enter the wiki, and start a subsection with your name for the title. Use the style *Heading 2* for the section head.
3. Create a sub-section, using the style *Heading 3* for the heading. Name the section today's date.
4. Enter observations about the plant's appearance, texture, smell, etc. **Do not taste the plant unless an experience, qualified forager has confirmed it is edible. Wash your hands after handling it.** Also record your observations about the area immediately around the plant: the soil, nearby plants, shade and sun..
5. Over the next few weeks, return to the workshop every few days to record changes on the plants and their immediate environment. Especially, record your observations after a significant weather event: rain, a dry spell, an unseasonable change in temperature, etc.

Continue

In this workshop, the student writes and updates some defined observations. These observations are then rated by other students in the course. When the student first enters the workshop, he or she sees directions for completing the workshop. After reading these directions, the student continues to the workshop submission form:

Notice the online word processor that the student uses to write the assignment. This gives the student basic WYSIWYG features. The same word processor appears when course creators create web pages, when students write Journal entries, and other times when a user is editing and formatting text.

At the top of the page, you can see that this workshop has opening and closing dates for submissions, and for assessments. It also has a maximum point value of 16. When the students assess each others' work, they will see the evaluation criteria and how many points each criterion is worth.

If you're able to read Step 5 in the workshop directions above, you can see that the student should return to this workshop every few days to update this assignment. To enable this, the course creator used a feature that allows students to resubmit workshops. The course creator could have chosen to allow a single submission, instead.

Assessing Other Students' Work

In the previous subsection you saw how a student submits an assignment to a workshop. After each of the students submits an assignment, the student is given a chance to assess other students' work. In the following screenshot, Student Number2 has just submitted an assignment, and now can assess Student 1's work. Student 2 would begin the assessment by clicking on the Assess link.

Current phase: Allow Submissions and Assessments
Start of submissions: Monday, October 3 2005, 09:30 AM (37 days 12 hours)
End of submissions: Tuesday, October 3 2006, 09:30 AM (327 days 11 hours)
Start of assessments: Monday, October 3 2005, 09:30 AM (37 days 12 hours)
End of assessments: Tuesday, October 3 2006, 09:30 AM (327 days 11 hours)

Maximum grade: 16 (Specimen Assessment Form)

Show Workshop Description
Please assess these Student Submissions

Submission Title	Action	Comment
Chamomile Growing in the Cracks of the Sidewalk	Assess	

Your assessments of work by your peers
No Assessments Done
Your Submissions

Submission Title	Action	Submitted	Assessments
Edible Weeds in my Lawn		Wednesday, November 9 2005, 09:59 PM	0

You are logged in as Student Number2 (Logout)

Under Your assessments of work by your peers, you can see that this user has not yet assessed anyone else's work. Under Your Submissions, you can see the title of this user's submission, and that no one has yet assessed the submission.

The Specimen Assessment Form at the top of the page displays the form that the student will use to assess others' work. However, it is a sample form, so it does not affect anyone's assessment.

Assess this submission ⊙

Assessment of Chamomile Growing in the Cracks of the Sidewalk

	Assessment Thursday, November 9 2006, 09:59 PM
Element 1:	Please comment on the variety of plants chosen by this student.
	Weight: 2.00

Select	Criterion
⦿	No variety.
○	A good variety of plants.
○	Outstanding variety.

Feedback:

Clicking the Assess link brings up the assessment form for Student 1's workshop submission. The current user, Student 2, uses this form to assess the work. The teacher will have the opportunity to grade Student 2's assessment of Student 1's workshop. So not only does Moodle give you the ability to grade students' work, but also the ability to grade their assessments of other students' work. Because Moodle emphasizes collaborative effort, there are several places where a teacher can grade students on the quality of their collaboration.

Editing Mode

Let us see what happens when you turn on the editing mode to make changes.

Normal versus Editing Mode

When an anonymous user or a registered student browses your learning site, Moodle displays pages normally. However, when someone with course creator privilege logs in, Moodle offers a button for switching into Editing mode:

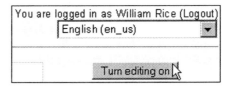

Clicking Turn editing on puts Moodle into Editing mode:

Normal Mode

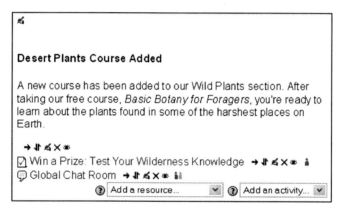

Editing Mode

The Edit Icon

Clicking the Edit icon ✍ enables you to edit whatever that icon follows. In this example, clicking the Edit icon that follows the paragraph enables you to edit the announcement.

Clicking the Edit icon next to the quiz Win a Prize, takes you into the editing window for that quiz. In that window, you can create, add, and remove quiz questions; change the grading scheme; and apply other settings to the quiz.

The Delete Icon

Clicking the Delete icon ✗ deletes whatever item that the icon follows. If you want to remove an item from a course, but you're not sure if you'll want to use it later, don't delete the item. Instead, hide it from view. Hiding and showing is explained next.

The Hidden/Shown Icons

I call these the Hidden/Shown icons ⊶ / 🐝 instead of Hide/Show because the icons indicate the current state of an item, instead of indicating what will happen when you click on them. The Hidden icon indicates that an item is hidden from the students. Clicking it shows the item to the students. The Show icon indicates that an item is shown for the students. Clicking it hides the item from the students.

If you want to remove an item from a course while keeping it for later use, or if you want to keep an item hidden from students while you're working on it, hide it instead of deleting it.

The Group Icons

These 🧍 👥 👥 icons indicate what Group Mode has been applied, to an item. Groups are explained in a later chapter. For now, you should know that you can control access to items based upon what Group a student belongs to. Clicking these icons enables you to change that setting.

Resources and Activities

Course materials that a student observes or reads—such as web or text pages, hyperlinks, and multimedia files—are called Resources. Now let us see how to add some Resources and Activities to your Moodle site.

In Editing Mode, you can add Resources and Activities to a course. In general, a Resource is an item that the student views but does not interact with, such as a web page, hyperlink, or directory of files. An Activity is an item that the student interacts with, or that enables interaction between students. Moodle offers more Activities than Resources, such as Chat, Forum, Journal, Quiz, Wiki, and more.

Adding Resources and Activities

You add Resources and Activities using the drop-down menus that appear in Editing Mode:

Add a resource...	Add an activity... ▾
Add a resource..	Add an activity..
Compose a text page	Assignment
Compose a web page	Chat
Link to a file or web site	Choice
Display a directory	Forum
Insert a label	Glossary
	Journal
	Lesson
	Questionnaire
	Quiz
	SCORM
	Survey
	Wiki
	Workshop

Link to a file or web site ⑦

Name: [   ]

Summary:

Summary ⑦

| Trebuchet ⌄ | 1 (8 pt) ⌄ | ⌄ | **B** *I* <u>U</u> S̶ | x₂ x² | 🗎 ✂ 🗎 ⚏ | ↶ ↷ |

| ☰ ⬚ | ☰ ☰ | ¶ ¶ | ☰ ☰ ⛭ ⛭ | 🄰 🄰 | — ⚓ ⊖ ⇔ ⇔ | 🖾 🖵 ☺ 🏵 🗎 ◇ 🖾 |

```



```
Path:

Location: [http://   ]

[Choose or upload a file ...] [Search for web page ...]

Window: [Hide settings] ⑦

    ◉ **Same window**

        ☑ Put resource in a frame to keep site navigation visible

    ○ **New window**

        ☑ Allow the window to be resized
        ☑ Allow the window to be scrolled
        ☑ Show the directory links
        ☑ Show the location bar
        ☑ Show the menu bar
        ☑ Show the toolbar
        ☑ Show the status bar
        [620] Default window width (in pixels)
        [450] Default window height (in pixels)

Selecting an item brings you to the Editing window for that type of item. For example, selecting Link to a file or web site displays the window above. Notice that you can do much more than just specify a hyperlink. You can give this link a user-friendly name and a summary description, open it in a new window, and more.

Almost every Resource and Activity that you add to Moodle has a Summary. This Summary appears when a student selects the item. Also, if the item appears in a list (for example, a list of all the Links in a course), the Summary is displayed.

When building courses, you will spend most of your time in the Editing windows for the items that you add. You will find their behavior and appearance to be very consistent. The presence of a Summary is one example of that consistency. Another example is the presence of the Help icon ⑦ next to the title of the window. Clicking this icon displays an explanation of this type of item.

The Administration Block

The Administration block displays only when someone with administration or course creator privileges has logged in. The choices on this block change according to whether you are viewing the Front Page or a course, and according to what privileges you have. The block on the left appears on the Front Page of my site. Notice that several choices appear to be for site-wide functions, such as Configuration, Courses, and Site files. Clicking the Admin link takes you to the Administration page for the entire site, which offers the choices on this block and more. The block on the right appears in a course on my site. Choices in this block affect only the current course. For example, selecting Logs from the Front Page displays a page where you can view logs for all site activity, while selecting it from the course displays logs for just that course.

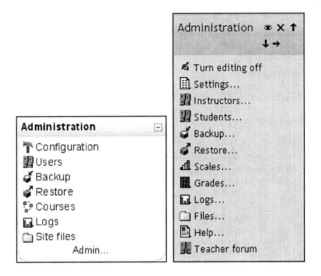

And Much More

This short tour introduced you to the basics of the Moodle experience. The following chapters take you through installing Moodle and creating courses. If you work through those chapters in order, you will discover many features not mentioned in this tour. And, because Moodle is open source, new features can be added at any time. Perhaps you will be the one to contribute a new feature to the Moodle community.

Without delay, let's get started building your site.

The Moodle Architecture

Moodle runs on any web server that supports the PHP programming language, and a database. It works best, and there is more support, when running on the Apache web server with a MySQL database. These requirements, Apache, PHP, and MySQL are common to almost all commercial web hosts, even the lowest-cost ones.

The Moodle learning management system resides in three places on your web host:

- The application occupies one directory, with many subdirectories for the various modules.

- Data files students and teachers upload—such as photos and assignments submitted by students—reside in the Moodle data directory.

- Course material that you create with Moodle (web pages, quizzes, workshops, lessons, etc.), grades, user information, and user logs reside in the Moodle database.

The Moodle Application Directory

The screenshot on the following page shows you my Moodle application directory. Without even knowing much about Moodle, you can guess the function of several directories. For example, the admin directory holds the PHP code that creates the administrative pages, the lang directory holds translations of the Moodle interface, and the mod directory holds the various modules:

Location: /www/moodle/moodle							
Select	Type	Permission	User	Group	Size	Date	Filename
←BACK							..
☐	🗀	drwxr-xr-x	williamr	williamr	4096	Sep 05 22:05	**admin**
☐	🗀	drwxr-xr-x	williamr	williamr	4096	May 24 02:03	**auth**
☐	🗀	drwxr-xr-x	williamr	williamr	4096	Sep 29 22:05	**backup**
☐	🗀	drwxr-xr-x	williamr	williamr	4096	Sep 29 22:05	**blocks**
☐	🗀	drwxr-xr-x	williamr	williamr	4096	Sep 29 22:05	**calendar**
☐	🗀	drwxr-xr-x	williamr	williamr	4096	Sep 23 22:05	**course**
☐	🗀	drwxr-xr-x	williamr	williamr	4096	Jun 18 22:11	**doc**
☐	🗀	drwxr-xr-x	williamr	williamr	4096	Sep 29 22:05	**enrol**
☐	🗀	drwxr-xr-x	williamr	williamr	4096	May 24 02:04	**error**
☐	🗀	drwxr-xr-x	williamr	williamr	4096	Sep 29 22:05	**files**
☐	🗀	drwxr-xr-x	williamr	williamr	4096	Sep 29 22:05	**filter**
☐	🗀	drwxr-xr-x	williamr	williamr	4096	Sep 27 22:05	**grade**
☐	🗀	drwxr-xr-x	williamr	williamr	4096	Sep 29 22:05	**lang**
☐	🗀	drwxr-xr-x	williamr	williamr	4096	Sep 29 22:05	**lib**
☐	🗀	drwxr-xr-x	williamr	williamr	4096	Sep 23 22:05	**login**
☐	🗀	drwxr-xr-x	williamr	williamr	4096	Sep 07 22:04	**message**
☐	🗀	drwxr-xr-x	williamr	williamr	4096	Oct 19 14:47	**mod**
☐	🗀	drwxr-xr-x	williamr	williamr	4096	May 24 02:07	**pix**
☐	🗀	drwxr-xr-x	williamr	williamr	4096	Sep 29 22:05	**rss**
☐	🗀	drwxr-xr-x	williamr	williamr	4096	Aug 01 22:25	**sso**
☐	🗀	drwxr-xr-x	williamr	williamr	4096	Sep 29 22:05	**theme**
☐	🗀	drwxr-xr-x	williamr	williamr	4096	Sep 28 22:04	**user**
☐	🗀	drwxr-xr-x	williamr	williamr	4096	May 24 02:07	**userpix**
☐	PHP	-rw-r--r--	williamr	williamr	15087	Jul 04 22:13	config-dist.php
☐	PHP	-rw-r-----	williamr	williamr	724	Sep 30 13:24	config.php
☐	PHP	-rw-r--r--	williamr	williamr	5931	Jul 12 22:16	file.php
☐	PHP	-rw-r--r--	williamr	williamr	4893	May 24 02:03	help.php
☐	PHP	-rw-r--r--	williamr	williamr	7529	May 24 02:03	index.php
☐	PHP	-rw-r--r--	williamr	williamr	23503	May 24 02:03	install.php
☐	📄	-rw-r--r--	williamr	williamr	943	May 24 02:03	README.txt
☐	📄	-rw-r--r--	williamr	williamr	2923484	Jul 06 02:09	tags
☐	PHP	-rw-r--r--	williamr	williamr	515	Sep 10 22:05	version.php

The index.php file is the Moodle home page. If a student were browsing my Moodle site, the first page the student would read is the file http://moodle.williamrice.com/index.php.

In my site, the free course "Basic Botany for Foragers" happens to be course number 4. Only the Moodle system knows it as course number 4; we know it as "Basic Botany for Foragers". When a student enters that course, the URL in the student's browser reads http://moodle.williamrice.com/moodle/course/view.php?id=4. In the previous screenshot above, you can see that /course is one of the directories in my Moodle installation. As the user navigates around the site, different .php pages do the work of presenting information.

Because each of Moodle's core components and modules is in its own subdirectory, the software can be easily updated by replacing old files with newer ones. You should periodically check the http://www.moodle.org website for news about updates and bug fixes.

The Moodle Data Directory

Moodle stores files uploaded by the users in a data directory. This directory should not be accessible to the general public over the Web. That is, you should not be able to type in the URL for this directory and access it using a web browser. You can protect it either by using an .htaccess file or by placing the directory outside the web server's documents directory.

In my installation, the previous screenshot shows you that the web document directory for moodle.williamrice.com is /www/moodle. Therefore, I placed the data directory outside of /www/moodle, in /www/moodledata:

Location: /www							
Select	Type	Permission	User	Group	Size	Date	Filen
	🗀	drwxrwxr-x	root	williamr	4096	Oct 24 14:45	**moodle**
	🗀	drwxrwxr-x	williamr	williamr	4096	Jul 11 16:45	**moodledata**
	🗀	drwxrwxr-t	williamr	williamr	4096	Mar 28 2005	**www**
	🗎	-rw-rwxr--	williamr	williamr	24	Aug 22 2003	.bash_logou
	🗎	-rw-rwxr--	williamr	williamr	191	Aug 22 2003	.bash_profil
	🗎	-rw-rwxr--	williamr	williamr	124	Aug 22 2003	.bashrc
	🗎	-rw-rwxr--	williamr	williamr	3511	Aug 22 2003	.screenrc

On my server, the directory /www/moodledata corresponds to the subdomain www.moodledata.williamrice.com. This subdomain is protected from open access by an .htaccess file. The directory /www/www corresponds to the root domain, www.williamrice.com.

The Moodle Database

While the Moodle data directory stores files uploaded by students, the Moodle database stores most of the information in your Moodle site. The database stores objects that you create using Moodle. For example, Moodle enables you to create web pages for your courses. These web pages' actual HTML code is stored in the database. Links that you add to a course, the settings and content of forums and Wikis, and quizzes created with Moodle are all examples of data stored in the Moodle database.

The three parts of Moodle—the *application*, *data directory*, and *database*—work together to create your learning site. Chapter 9 talks about backing up and disaster recovery, which is an obvious application of this knowledge. However, knowing how the three parts work together is also helpful when upgrading, troubleshooting, and moving your site between servers.

Summary

Moodle encourages exploration and interaction between/among students and teachers. As a course designer and teacher, you will have the most tools at your disposal if you work with this tendency, and make your learning experiences as interactive as possible. Creating courses with forums, peer-assessed workshops, journals, surveys, and interactive lessons is more work than creating a course from a series of static web pages. However, it is also more engaging and effective, and you will find it worth the effort to use Moodle's many interactive features.

When teaching an online course in Moodle, remember that Moodle enables you to add, move, and modify course material and grading tools on-the-fly. If it's permitted by your institution's policies, don't hesitate to change a course in response to student needs.

Finally, learn the basics of Moodle's architecture, and at least read over the *Installation and Configuration* in Chapter 2. Don't be afraid of the technology. If you can master the difficult art of teaching, you can master using Moodle to its full potential.

2
Installing and Configuring Moodle

The title of this chapter makes it sound as if it applies only to the person who installs Moodle. If your system administrator or webmaster has installed Moodle for you, you might be tempted to skip this chapter. *Don't!*

Many of the configuration choices that are made during the installation process affect the student and teacher experience in Moodle. These are found on the Variables and Site Settings pages, which will be covered later in this chapter. This chapter's focus is on helping you create the user experience you want by making the right configuration choices. While someone else may have installed Moodle and made these configuration choices for you, you can always go back and change them.

Go Ahead, Experiment

While this chapter describes the effects of different configuration choices, there is no substitute for experiencing them yourself. Don't be afraid to experiment with different settings. You can try this method:

1. Install two different browsers in your computer. For example, **Internet Explorer** and **Firefox**.

2. In one browser, log in as an *administrator*. Go to the Site Settings or Variables page (I will tell you how), and experiment with the settings that you read about here.

3. In the other browser, go to your site as a *user*—an anonymous visitor, student, or teacher. Each time you change a configuration setting, refresh the user's browser and observe the change to your site.

Using This Chapter

If you did not install Moodle, you should at least read the following sections later in this chapter:

- *Installation Step 7d: Specify Site Variables.* The site variables described affect how the site functions. Some of them affect the user experience, and others affect the teachers and course creators.

- *Configuration Choices after Installation.* Most of these configuration choices affect the student experience, and some affect the teachers and course creators.

- If you want, work with your system administrator to select the settings you want. Your administrator can create a site administrator account that you can use for this.

Moodle's online installation instructions provide a good step-by-step reference for installing Moodle. However, they do not cover the implications of the choices you make while configuring Moodle. This chapter covers the effects of the:

- Choices you make while installing Moodle

- Choices you make immediately after installing Moodle

- Ways of authenticating Moodle users, and how your choice affects the operation of your site

Accessing the Site Variables and Site Settings Pages

The fastest way to access the Variables and Site Settings pages is to:

1. Log in to Moodle with an administrator account.
2. In your browser bar, enter the URL of your site and add /admin. For example, moodle.williamrice.com/admin.
3. The Administration page displays. From here, you can select Variables or Site Settings.

Administration	
Configuration	Variables – Configure variables that affect general operation of the site
	Site settings – Define how the front page of the site looks
	Themes – Choose how the site looks (colors, fonts etc)
	Language – For checking and editing the current language pack
	Modules – Manage installed modules and their settings
	Blocks – Manage installed blocks and their settings
	Filters – Choose text filters and related settings
	Backup – Configure automated backups and their schedule
	Editor settings – Define basic settings for HTML editor
Users	Authentication – You can use internal user accounts or external databases
	Edit user accounts – Browse the list of user accounts and edit any of them
	Add a new user – To manually create a new user account
	Upload users – Import new user accounts from a text file
	Enrolments – Choose internal or external ways to control enrolments
	Enroll students – Go into a course and add students from the admin menu
	Assign teachers – Find a course then use the icon to add teachers ⊛
	Assign creators – Creators can create new courses and teach in them
	Assign admins – Admins can do anything and go anywhere in the site
Courses	Define courses and categories and assign people to them
Logs	Browse logs of all activity on this site
Site files	For publishing general files or uploading external backups

Installing Moodle

Installing Moodle consists of:

1. Obtaining space and rights on a web server that has the capabilities needed to run Moodle
2. Creating the subdomains and/or directories needed for Moodle and its data
3. Getting and unpacking Moodle, and uploading it to your web server
4. Creating the data directory
5. Creating the Moodle database
6. Setting up the cron job
7. Activating the installation routine and specifying settings for your Moodle site

Each of these is covered in the following sections.

The official Moodle website, `http://moodle.org/`, contains detailed installation instructions. These instructions might change slightly with each version, or be occasionally updated. The material in this chapter supplements and expands on those directions. You should use the official Moodle installation directions, supplemented with this material.

Installation Step 1: The Web Server

Moodle is run from a web server. You upload or place Moodle in your directory on the server. Usually, the server is someone else's computer. If you're a teacher, or are in the corporate world, your institution might have their own web server. If you're an individual or have a small business, you will probably buy web-hosting services from another company. In either case, we are assuming that you have an account on a web server that offers Apache, PHP, and MySQL. If you must install your own Apache web server and MySQL software, the easiest way to do so is to use another open-source tool: XAMPP from `http://www.apachefriends.org`. Apache Friends is a non-profit project to promote the Apache web server. XAMPP is an easy, all-in-one installer that installs Apache, MySQL, PHP, and Perl. It is available for Linux, Windows, Mac, and Solaris.

How Much Hosting Service Do You Need?

With only a few dozen students, Moodle runs fine on a modest web-hosting service. At this time, many hosting companies offer services that can run a small Moodle installation for less than $10 a month. Base your decision upon the factors discussed below.

Disk Space

A fresh Moodle installation will occupy about 60MB of disk space, which is not much. Most of the space will be occupied by content that is added while users create and take courses. Base your decision about how much space to obtain upon the kinds of courses you plan to deliver. If the courses will contain mostly text and a few graphics, you'll need less space than if they contain music and video files. Also, consider the disk space occupied by files that the students will upload. Will students upload small word processing files? Large graphics? Huge multimedia files? When determining how much disk space you will need, consider the size of the files that your courses will serve and that your students will submit.

Bandwidth

Moodle is a web-based product, so course content and assignments are added over the Web. Whenever a reader or user connects to a website, they're using bandwidth. When a user reads a page on your Moodle site, downloads a video, or uploads a paper, he or she uses some of your bandwidth. Most commercial hosting services include a fixed amount of bandwidth in their service. If your account uses more bandwidth than allowed, some services cut off your site's access. Others keep your site up, but automatically bill you for the additional bandwidth. The second option is preferable in case of unexpected demand. When deciding upon a hosting service, find out how much bandwidth they offer and what they do if you exceed that limit.

Installation Step 2: Subdomains

A subdomain is a web address that exists under your web address, and acts like an independent site. For example, my website is www.williamrice.com. I have a subdomain, http://www.moodle.williamrice.com, which holds a demonstration site for this book. They are independent sites. However, they exist on the same server, under the same account, and they both count towards the disk space and bandwidth that I use:

In this example, Moodle is installed in the subdomain http://www.moodle.williamrice.com. Using a subdomain offers me several advantages. As you can see, I can manage them both from the same interface. Second, I can use a subdomain as a test site for my Moodle installation. I can install and test Moodle in the subdomain, and then copy it over to my main site when it's ready. Having a site to test updates and add-ons may be helpful if uninterrupted service is important to you. Later, you'll see how easy it is to copy a Moodle installation to a different location, change a few settings, and have it work. If you want to do this, make sure the hosting service you choose allows subdomains.

Installation Step 3: Getting and Unpacking Moodle

Get Moodle from the official website, `http://www.moodle.org/`. Go to the Download Moodle page and select the version and format that you need:

Which Version?

For a new installation, the Latest Stable Branch is usually your best choice. The Last build: information tells you when it was last updated with a bug-fix or patch. This is usually irrelevant to you; the version number determines which features you get, not the build time.

Which Format?

Moodle is downloaded as a single, compressed file. This compressed file contains the many small files and directories that constitute Moodle. After downloading the compressed file, you must decompress (or unzip) the file. Unzipping will extract many files and directories that you must place on your server.

If you're using a hosting service, you probably do not have the ability to decompress the file on the server. Instead, you must decompress the file on your PC and then upload the extracted files to the server. If you're using a hosting service, you will probably:

1. Download the Moodle package (ZIP file) to your local hard drive.

	Version / CVS tag	Date	Information	.tgz format	.zip format
Latest Stable Branch	Moodle 1.4.4+ MOODLE_14_STABLE	Built daily	The 1.4 stable branch is continually being patched with new bug fixes since the last release, but no new features. It is a usually a good choice for a new server, but you may want the certainty of a definite release like 1.4.4. Last build: 1 hour 35 mins ago.	Download	Download
Latest Stable Release	Moodle 1.4.4 MOODLE_144	9th March 2005	The last stable reference release that was distributed wide. Read the release notes here.		
Previous Stable Branch	Moodle 1.3.5 MOODLE_13_STABLE	Built daily	Stable, but old now and missing many of the new feat Mostly useful for those maintaining 1.3.x servers.		

Open
Open in New Window
Save Target As...
Print Target
Cut
Copy
Copy Shortcut
Paste

2. Decompress, or unzip, the package. This will extract many files from the package. In the example overleaf, you can see from the title bar that I'm using the freeware program **ZipGenius** to unzip the package. Each file will be extracted to a specific directory. For example, near the bottom of the window, you can see that the file module.php will be extracted to the directory moodle\admin\.

3. Upload the files to your web server. You'll need to use a special program to upload the files, which we'll cover later. In this example, I'm using **Macromedia Dreamweaver** to upload the file help.php from my local PC to my hosting service.

Whether you're using Windows, Mac, or Linux on your personal computer, you can find a decompression program that will unzip .zip files. If your system doesn't have a decompression program that works with .zip files, and you're using Windows, try www.nonags.com for freeware unzip programs. If you're using a web page editor like Dreamweaver or Microsoft FrontPage, your program has the ability to upload files to the server. If you're not using a web page editor that can upload files, you'll need an "FTP client". Again, try www.nonags.com for freeware FTP clients.

If your school or company has given you space on its web server, you might have access to the directory just as if it were another folder on your PC. In that case, you can download the .tgz file, put it into your directory on the web server, and then decompress it. Tell the system administrator who gave you access what you want to do, and ask how to decompress a file in your directory.

Installation Step 4: The Moodle Data Directory

When you run the Moodle install script, the installer asks you to specify a directory in which to store course material. For security, this directory should be outside the main Moodle directory. This gives you two choices:

- You can install Moodle into a subdirectory, and the data into another subdirectory. For example, suppose your domain is www.williamrice.com. Your Moodle site might be located in www.williamrice.com/moodle, and the data at www.williamrice.com/moodledata.

- Alternatively, you can install Moodle into its own domain, and the data into another domain. For example, if you own the domain www.williamrice.com, you could create a subdomain for Moodle at www.moodle.williamrice.com and a subdomain for the course materials at www.moodledata.williamrice.com. This is usually the easiest option.

The two screenshots below illustrate this setup. The screen on the left is when I used my hosting service's control panel to create the moodledata subdirectory. The screen on the right appears while the configuration script runs. By entering /home/williamr/www/moodle, I specified the subdomain http://moodle.williamrice.com as the Moodle Directory. /home/williamr/www/moodledata specifies the subdomain, http://moodledata.williamrice.com as the Data Directory:

Installation Step 5: Creating the Moodle Database

While the moodledata directory stores files uploaded by students, and some larger files, the Moodle database stores most of the information in your Moodle site. By default, the installer uses the database name moodle and the username **moodleuser**. Using these default settings gives any hacker a head start on breaking your site. When creating your database, change these to something less common. At least make the hackers guess the name of your database and the database username.

Control Panel » MySQL Data Base	
DATABASE MANAGER	
DB Master Username: williamr	
User williamr has 3 of 4 maximum allowed DBs.	
You can manipulate your DBs with **phpMyAdmin**	

Databases

DB Name:	Remove/Import:
learn	[Del] [Import]
mambo	[Del] [Import]
moodledata	[Del] [Import]

Database name: [_____] **Create**

MySQL users

DB Name:	Subuser:	Privileges:	Remote Connections:
learn	lms [Del]	Select, Insert, Update, Delete, Create, Drop, Alter, Lock	Enabled [Disable]
learn	williamr	Master user	Enabled [Disable]
mambo	mambouser [Del]	Select, Insert, Update, Delete, Create, Alter, Lock	Enabled [Disable]
mambo	williamr	Master user	Enabled [Disable]
moodledata	moodleusr [Del]	Select, Insert, Update, Delete, Create, Drop, Alter,	Enabled [Disable]
moodledata	williamr	Master user	Enabled [Disable]

Whatever username you use, that user will need the following privileges for the Moodle database: SELECT, INSERT, UPDATE, DELETE, CREATE, DROP, INDEX, and ALTER. The screenshot here shows the settings for my demo Moodle database, moodledata. If your hosting service provides you with the popular cPanel control panel for your account, you can use cPanel to create the database and database user. For instructions on using cPanel, see http://www.cpanel.net/docs/cpanel/.

Installation Step 6: Setting up the Cron Job

Some of Moodle's functions happen on a regular, timed schedule. The most visible example is mailing out notices to the subscribers of a forum that a new message has been posted. A script called `cron.php` checks periodically to see if new messages have been posted to any forum. If so, the script causes the notice to be emailed to the members of that forum.

The script `cron.php` must be triggered at regular intervals. You can set this interval. The mechanism that triggers the script is called a **cron job**. Directions for setting up the cron job are in the `http://moodle.org/` installation guide.

Some web-hosting services allow you to set up cron jobs. If you're buying hosting services, look for one that offers this. If you've been given space on your school's or company's web server, speak to the system administrator about setting up the cron job. If neither of these applies, then your only other option is to set up the cron job on a Windows machine that you control. The cron job will reach out over the Internet to your Moodle site, and activate the script `cron.php`. Again, directions for this are in the `http://moodle.org/` installation guide. However, if you choose this option, you must keep that Windows PC running all the time, and it must also be connected to the Internet at all times. If the Windows PC goes down or offline, the Moodle functions that requires periodic triggering will also go down.

The following is a screenshot of installing the MoodleCron application, where I specify the location of the `cron.php` script. In the following figure, you can see the line Location: /www/moodle/admin, which on my server corresponds to `www.moodle.williamrice.com/admin`. This is the directory that holds `cron.php`.

Installation Step 7: The Installer Script

The installer script walks you step by step through the creation of Moodle's database tables, and setting variables that determine how the site operates. In this section, we discuss how the setting of each variable affects the user experience.

Installation Step 7a: Run install.php

In the Moodle directory, a script called install.php creates the Moodle configuration file when the script is run. You run the script by just launching your browser and calling the script. The configuration file, config.php, holds information about your Moodle installation.

In the following screenshot, I've launched my browser and accessed install.php on my server:

Installation Step 7b: Specify Settings for config.php

Stepping through the install routine creates config.php, among other things. Here's the config.php for www.moodle.williamrice.com:

```php
<?php  /// Moodle Configuration File

unset($CFG);

$CFG->dbtype    = 'mysql';
$CFG->dbhost    = 'localhost';
$CFG->dbname    = 'moodledata';
$CFG->dbuser    = 'moodleusr';
$CFG->dbpass    = 'badpassword';
$CFG->dbpersist =  false;
$CFG->prefix    = 'mdl_';

$CFG->wwwroot   = 'http://moodle.williamrice.com';
```

```
$CFG->dirroot    = '/home/williamr/www/moodle';
$CFG->dataroot   = '/home/williamr/www/moodledata';
$CFG->admin      = 'admin';

$CFG->directorypermissions = 00777;   // try 02777 on a server in Safe
Mode

require_once("$CFG->dirroot/lib/setup.php");
// MAKE SURE WHEN YOU EDIT THIS FILE THAT THERE ARE NO SPACES, BLANK
LINES,
// RETURNS, OR ANYTHING ELSE AFTER THE TWO CHARACTERS ON THE NEXT
LINE.
?>
```

This site uses a mysql database. On most servers, the hostname will be localhost. In a previous subsection we covered creating the Moodle database, which in our example we called moodledata. We created a user called moodleusr, with the proper privileges. Note that the configuration file stores the password for the Moodle database, which in this example is badpassword. The dbpersist setting is specified by the installer script; do not change it without a good reason.

The prefix mdl_ is added to the beginning of each table that Moodle adds to your database. A table is a section of a database. Think of each table as a database inside a database. On the running of install.php, Moodle adds all the tables it needs to the database that you created. It adds the prefix to the name of each of these tables, so that you (and Moodle) can recognize them when you look at the database. You could use the same database for Moodle and something else, or for two Moodle installations, if each program used its own tables with its own prefix. The different prefixes would prevent the two programs from becoming confused and reading each other's tables. If you're running more than one copy of Moodle, you might consider using the same database and different tables. You could back up the data for both copies by backing up the one database.

The settings in the first part of config.php are specified while running the installation script:

The second part of config.php specifies the directories used by the Moodle application and data:

```
$CFG->wwwroot    = 'http://moodle.williamrice.com';
$CFG->dirroot    = '/home/williamr/www/moodle';
$CFG->dataroot   = '/home/williamr/www/moodledata';
$CFG->admin      = 'admin';
```

These settings are also specified while running the installation script:

Installation Step 7c: Database Tables Created by install.php

After stepping through a few more screens, install.php creates the tables in your Moodle database. You don't need to do anything during this part of the installation except click to see the next screen. The installation script tells you when this is complete:

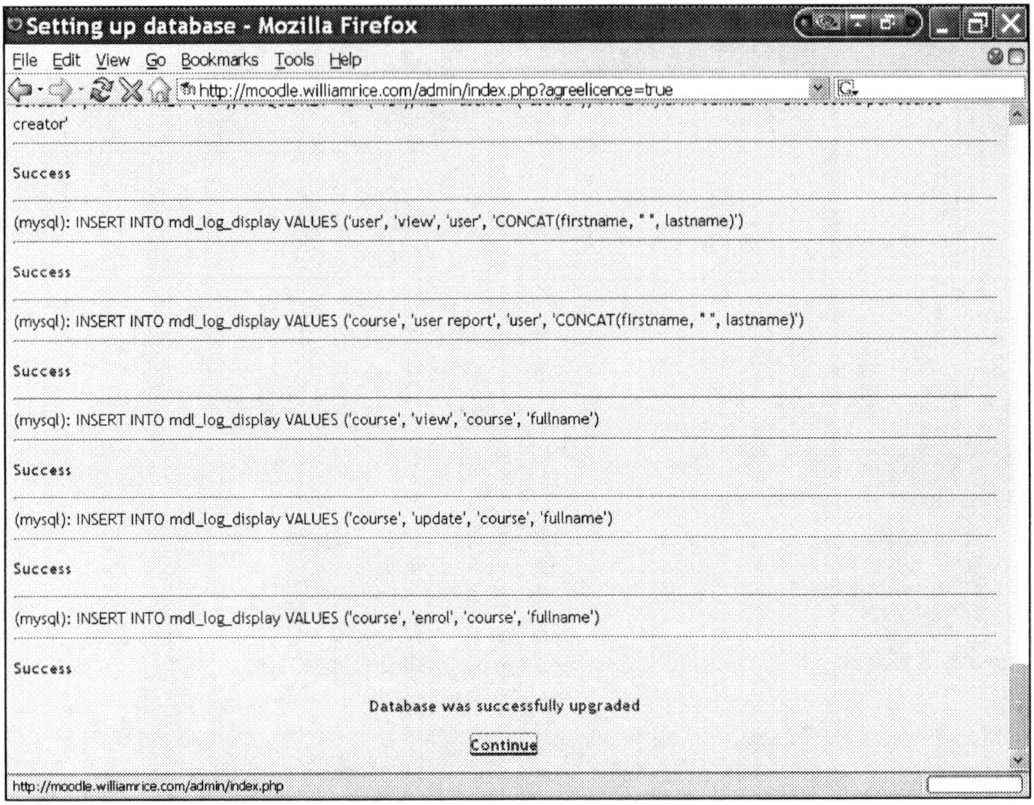

Installation Step 7d: Specify Site Variables

After creating the database tables, the installation script displays the Variables page. The values you enter on this page affect the behavior of the entire site. Of course, you want to enter them correctly the first time. However, after Moodle is installed, you can return to this page at any time to change these variables.

The next screenshot shows the top of the Variables page for my demonstration site. Notice the breadcrumbs line at the top shows that I'm on the site whose short name is wildskills, and that to get to this page I've selected Administration, then Configuration, and then Variables:

The page itself does a good job of explaining the purpose of each variable. However, the directions do not tell you the implications of the choices you make on this page. Below I've added some commentary to help you determine how your choices will affect the operation of your site, and information to help you decide upon the right choices for your needs.

lang and langmenu

The default language is specified by the variable lang. This is the language users will see when they first encounter your site. The variable langmenu determines whether users will see a language menu on your Front Page:

Notice that the site title, in this case Wilderness Skills, does not get translated. Neither does the content that you create. Only menus and field names are translated. In this example, Main menu, Site news, and Subscribe to this forum would be translated.

If you want to offer course content in multiple languages, you have several choices. First, you could put all of the different languages into each course. That is, each document would appear in a course in several languages. For example, if you offered a botany course in English and Spanish, you might have a document defining the different types of plants in both English and Spanish, side by side in the same course: Types of Plants or Tipos de Plantaras. While taking the course, students would select the documents in their language. Course names would appear in only one language.

Second, you could create separate courses for each language, and offer them on the same site. Course names would appear in each language. In this case, students would select the course in English or Spanish: Basic Botany or Botánica Básica.

Third, you could create a separate Moodle site for each language. For example, http://moodle.williamrice.com/english and http://moodle.williamrice.com/spanish. At the home page of your site, students would select their language and be directed to the correct Moodle installation. In this case, the entire Moodle site would appear in the students' language: the site name, menus, course names, and course content. These are things you should consider before installing Moodle. However, if you decide to change your approach, you can always come back to the Variables page and change these settings.

Fourth, and most elegantly, you could use the Multi-Language Content filter described in *Configuration Choices after Installation* later in this chapter to display course content in the language selected by your user.

langlist

As the directions on the Variables page state, leaving this blank will enable your students to pick from all available languages. Entering the names of languages in this field limits the list to only those entered. The directions tell you to enter "language codes".

Moodle looks in the /lang directory for subdirectories that hold each language's files. For example, the /lang/en_us subdirectory holds files for the U.S. English translation, and /lang/es_es holds the files for traditional Spanish (Español / España). The name of the subdirectory is the "language code." For example, if you want students to be able to choose between U.S. English and traditional Spanish, enter en_us, es_es into this field.

For example, the /lang/en/forum.php file holds text used on the forum pages. This includes text that is displayed to the course creator when creating the forum, and text that is displayed to the students when they use the forum. Here are the first few lines from that file:

```
$string['addanewdiscussion'] = 'Add a new discussion topic';
$string['addanewtopic'] = 'Add a new topic';
$string['advancedsearch'] = 'Advanced search';
```

```
And here are the same first three lines from /lang/es_es/forum.php:
$string['addanewdiscussion'] = 'Colocar un nuevo tema de discusión
aquí';
$string['addanewtopic'] = 'Agregar un nuevo tema';
$string['advancedsearch'] = 'Búsqueda avanzada';
```

The biggest task in localizing Moodle consists of translating these language files into the appropriate language. Some translations are surprisingly complete. For example, most of the interface has been translated to **Irish Gaelic**, even though this language is used daily by only about 350,000 people; the Romanian interface remains mostly untranslated, while Romania has a population of over 23 million. This means that if a Moodle user chooses the Romanian language (ro), most of the interface will still default to English.

One of the greatest features of Moodle is that you can edit these language files directly in Moodle. To do this, select Administration | Configuration | Language. For more information about translating Moodle, see http://docs.moodle.org/en/Translation.

locale

Enter a language code into this field, and the system displays dates in the format appropriate for that language.

timezone

This field determines the time zone for times displayed, such as the last time a file was edited. The time zone entered here is used only for users who have not selected a time zone in their personal profile. Once a user selects a time zone for their profile, times are displayed in the user's time zone.

country

Leaving this field blank forces a new student to choose a country on the student's profile page. This could either be interesting or inconvenient for the students. Consider your students' temperament before making your selection.

smtphosts, smtpuser, and smtppass

The abbreviation SMTP stands for **Simple Mail Transfer Protocol**. It's a protocol, or communications method, used between computers. It describes the method those computers use to exchange email. To find out the name of the SMTP host to use, consult your hosting service or system administrator. It is usually mail@domainname, for example mail@williamrice.com.

The SMTP username is the first part of a valid email address, on the same server as Moodle. Your hosting service probably allows you to create multiple email addresses. On my hosting service, I created an email address moodle@williamrice.com. The smtpuser field contains moodle and the smtppass field contains that email address's password.

noreplyaddress

This email address is used as the "reply to" address when Moodle sends an email to which you don't want a response. For example, Moodle can email the members of a forum when a new post is added to the forum. You would not want the members to respond to that notice by using "reply to," because the email comes from Moodle, not an individual who can read the replies. That is one of the times Moodle would use this `noreplyaddress`.

If you have a catch-all email address for your domain, replies sent to `noreplyaddress` will be caught by the catch-all address. For example, if I designate `catchall@williamrice.com` as the catch-all email address for my domain, any message sent to an invalid email address at `williamrice.com` gets caught by `catchall@williamrice.com`. If you don't have a catch-all email address for your domain, messages sent to `noreplyaddress` will be bounced.

gdversion

GD is a collection of open-source programs that can generate graphics, charts, and thumbnails on the fly. This library is installed on your web server. Most hosting services will have the latest version installed. Moodle uses GD to process images. The installation routine usually detects the correct version of GD installed on your server. However, if images do not display properly, try returning to this page and changing the setting. Also contact your system administrator and ask what version of GD is installed.

maxeditingtime

This sets the amount of time between when a forum posting or journal entry is submitted, and when it is added to the forum or journal. During this time, the posting or entry can be recalled by the author and edited.

As of this writing, Moodle does not have a function specifically for sending emails to all the students in a course. When a teacher wants to send an email to all students in a course, the teacher usually creates a forum and automatically subscribes all students to that forum. Then, the teacher chooses to have new forum postings emailed to all the members. When the teacher posts to the forum, the forum then emails that posting to all the students. The `maxeditingtime` determines how long the teacher has before that posting is added to the forum and emailed to all the students.

longtimenosee

The maximum amount of time you can keep a student enrolled in a course is 1000 days. If you plan on keeping students enrolled longer than that, you'll need to modify Moodle's source code:

1. If you've already installed Moodle, select any value for this field.
2. In the directory /admin, open the file `config.htm`.
3. Look for the line `$options[1000]=get_string("numdays", "", 1000);`
4. In both places in that line, replace 1000 with the number of days to keep students enrolled.

5. Save `config.htm`.
6. Return to the Variables page by logging into Moodle as the administrator, and selecting Administration | Configuration | Variables.
7. For `longtimenosee`, select the value you entered into `config.htm`. You should see it in the pull-down list.
8. Save and exit the Variables page.

deleteunconfirmed

Students need an account on your site before they can enroll in a course. If you're using email to authenticate students, this sets the length of time they have to respond to the email. Note that while waiting for a student to respond to the authentication email, the username and email address of that student cannot be used by any other student. So, if a student loses the enrollment email, he or she should either wait until this time has expired or try again with a different username and email address.

If a student loses the enrollment email and must use the username and email address in that email, you will need to go into the Moodle database and delete the student's record. Look in the table called `mdl_user` for the username. You should see that the field `confirmed` contains a 0 (zero). Delete this record and have the student try enrolling again. You'll need to know how to edit a database to do this.

loglifetime

This sets the length of time Moodle keeps log files. Note that it doesn't set a size limit. If you have a very busy site, the log can become large quickly. Unlike most web-based programs that keep logs, Moodle does not keep them in their own files on the server. Instead, Moodle keeps log files in the Moodle database, in the table called `mdl_log`. This means that your database server must handle both Moodle content and logs. If you have a very active site and a very modest database server, or modest hosting service, this can slow down your site.

Consider setting `loglifetime` to the lowest value that you need to manage your courses. For example, if no course is longer than two weeks, 30 days of logs will usually give you enough time to look back at course activity. You can back up `mdl_log` to a local disk periodically, so that you can see archived course activity. You'll need to know how to edit a database to do this.

displayloginfailures, notifyloginfailures, and notifyloginthreshold

The settings you choose for these fields depend upon how closely you intend to monitor security on your site. There is very little drawback to choosing to display login failures to the administrator and teachers. If you're hosting courses that use an enrollment key, and students have trouble using the key to log in, `displayloginfailures` can give the administrator and teachers a warning that something is wrong.

For notifyloginfailures to work correctly, the persons being notified must have entered valid email addresses. The setting notifyloginthreshold will cause the system to send an email each time that threshold is reached. If you have this set to 10 failed logins, and your site becomes the target of an automated attack, this could result in a lot of emails clogging your inbox.

sessioncookie

If you're running several copies of Moodle from the same site, you can use this to customize the name of the cookie for each copy of Moodle. This prevents each copy of Moodle from using the other's cookie. For example, suppose I had one copy of Moodle running under www.williamrice.com/paid and another running under www.williamrice.com/free. I would not want the cookie set by the copy running under /free to be used by the copy running under /paid.

If you're running each copy of Moodle in a different subdomain, you don't need to customize the name of the session cookie. For example, if I was running different copies of Moodle under paid.williamrice.com and free.williarmrice.com, this setting would be unnecessary.

zip and unzip

The zip and unzip routines are used to compress entire courses before downloading them, and to uncompress them after uploading them. When you move a course between Moodle sites, or when you want to duplicate an entire course, the usual method is zip-download-upload-unzip.

If you think that you will frequently move courses between sites, or duplicate courses, then check with your hosting company to see if they offer this feature. Access to a zip and unzip program might be one of the factors in deciding which hosting service to use.

If your hosting service doesn't offer a zip program, then Moodle will use its own, built-in zip program. This uses a lot of memory, so you're always better off using your hosting service's zip program.

slasharguments

You need to change this only if you have trouble viewing uploaded graphics. Try running your site before changing this setting.

proxyhost and proxyport

Most web servers do not run from behind a firewall, especially paid hosting services. However, if you're hosting Moodle from a personal computer located inside a school or company, there's a good chance you're behind a firewall. For example, if you're hosting Moodle from a computer located at your desk in your school or company, then that host is probably behind the same firewall as every other personal computer in your institution. If this is the case, ask your network administrator for the setting to use in these fields.

If you're hosting Moodle from a personal computer inside your institution, not only might you need to deal with a firewall but also with a changing IP address. The IP address of that computer might change each time your reboot it. This would change the IP address that students use to access your site.

If you're running Moodle from a personal computer located inside your institution, ask your network administrator about the proxyhost settings and also if your Moodle server can have a fixed IP address.

framename

This feature is useful if you're embedding Moodle inside another site. For example, you may want to embed Moodle into your school's or company's pages, retaining the headers and footers used by your institution. If you embed Moodle like this, consider modifying the content of Moodle's headers and footers so they do not conflict with the information in your institution's headers and footers. You will find the files, header.html and footer.html in the folder /themes/themename, where themename is the name of the theme you chose under Administration | Configuration | Themes.

secureforms

Selecting Yes for this setting may cause pages to become unusable for students running firewalls. It gives you a small amount of additional security. If you turn this on, I suggest that you put a notice on your Login Page that the site may not work with a firewall when the firewall strips the IP address, or HTTP_REFERER, from the user's computer.

loginhttps

If you select Yes for this setting, but your server doesn't have HTTPS enabled for your site, you will be locked out of your site. Moodle will require you to use HTTPS when you log in, but you won't be able to comply. If that happens to you, then you must go into the Moodle database and change this setting to No.

The following screenshot shows an administrator using the web-based product phpMyAdmin to edit this setting in Moodle's database. Notice the setting for logging in via HTTPS is contained in the table mdl_config. The administrator is clicking on the edit icon. If this cell contains a 0, HTTPS login is not required. If it contains a 1, HTTPS login is required. If you're locked out because of HTTPS login, change the contents of this cell to 0.

allusersaresitestudents

The Front Page of your Moodle site can contain the same features as any other course. In fact, the Front Page can act as an introductory course to your site. It can contain forums, resources for students to read, quizzes, and other course material. Building a course on the Front Page of your site can be useful in two ways.

First, you can use the Front Page as a sample course for your site. The Front Page course becomes a sales tool. This is a good way to tempt new visitors into joining your site.

Alternatively, you can use the Front Page as an introductory course for existing students. This course would teach students how to use your site, how to choose and join courses, your policies and procedures. The Front Page course becomes an orientation.

The setting for allusersaresitestudents determines whether everyone who is a student (all registered users) is automatically enrolled in the Front Page course. If you're using the Front Page as a sample or orientation, you probably want this set to Yes.

showsiteparticipantslist

This setting determines whether students who are enrolled in the Front Page course (the "site course") are shown on the list of students for that course. Remember that if you set allusersaresitestudents to Yes, then all registered students are in the site course, and on this list.

Setting showsiteparticipantslist to Site teachers means that only teachers who teach the site course can see the list of students. Setting it to Students and teachers means that the students can see each others' name on this list. If all registered students are enrolled in the site course, then they can all see each others' name.

maxbytes

There are three settings that limit the size of a file that can be uploaded on your server. The first two are the PHP setting upload_max_filesize and the Apache setting LimitRequestBody. These are set by your hosting service. They are probably greater than the 20 Megabyte maximum that you can set with maxbytes. However, if you set this and then cannot upload files of the size you selected, talk to your system administrator or hosting service provider about their settings for upload_max_filesize and LimitRequestBody.

fullnamedisplay

Remember that your students may not want their full names displayed to one another. Consider privacy issues when selecting this setting.

autologinguests

When a course is created, the course creator can choose to allow guest access. If this is enabled, when a visitor who is not logged in selects the course, the visitor is taken to Moodle's Login Page. At the Login Page, one of the visitor's options is to Login as a guest. The visitor can then take the course anonymously, using the username guest.

If autologinguests is set to Yes, when a visitor who is not logged in chooses a course with guest access enabled, the visitor is taken straight into the course. The Moodle Login Page is bypassed, and the visitor does not need to register or select Login as a guest. This seems very convenient; however, you should consider how this might affect your registered users before enabling it.

With autologinguests set to No, when any course is selected, the visitor is taken to the Login Page. If the visitor is a registered student, he or she will login with a username/password. Then that visitor's activity in the guest-enabled course will be logged. However, if autologinguests is set to Yes, when a registered student hits your site and selects a guest-enabled course, the student will bypass the Login Page and be taken straight into the course. This means the student's activity will not be logged. If having a registered student take a course without logging the student's activity is OK, then enable autologinguests. However, if you want to be certain that all of your registered students' activities are logged, then you should disable this feature.

forcelogin

As stated in the directions, setting this to Yes causes the Front Page to become hidden until a visitor logs in to Moodle. When visitors first hit your Moodle site, they see the Moodle Login Page.

Setting this to Yes means that you cannot use Moodle's Front Page as an information and sales tool. You can customize the text on the Login Page, but you won't be able to add all the features available to a Moodle course.

Setting this to No enables you to use a non-Moodle page as your introduction to the site. If you want your Front Page to be something that cannot be created in Moodle, this is a good option. For example, you might make moodle.williamrice.com/index.htm into a flash presentation about your site. Visitors then click on an Enter link and are taken to the Moodle Login Page at moodle.williamrice.com/moodle/index.php. Notice that Moodle is now in its own subdirectory.

If you want a non-Moodle introduction page that leads to a Moodle Login Page, put Moodle into its own subdirectory and not in the same directory as the introduction page. Moodle's Front Page is called index.php, and your introduction page will probably be called index.htm. If they are in the same directory, your server might get confused about which page to serve.

forceloginforprofiles

What the directions don't state is that setting this to No enables anonymous visitors to read not only teachers' profiles, but also the profiles of any students enrolled in courses that have guest access. This may be a privacy issue.

The effect of enabling forceloginforprofiles is that anonymous visitors cannot read the profiles for the teachers in a course that accepts guest access. They must register as a student before being able to read student and user profiles. This may be a drawback if your teachers' profiles are a selling point for the course.

Consider enabling forceloginforprofiles to force people to register before reading student or teacher profiles. Then, if your teachers' profiles are a selling point, you can add a section to the Front Page for "About Our Teachers".

opentogoogle

This setting lets the Google indexing robot into a course that allows guest access. If you want to know more about the **Googlebot**, see http://www.google.com/bot.html.

It seems that everyone with a website wants their site to be ranked high in Google's search results. However, you should consider whether you really want Google to add each of your guest-enabled courses to its search engine. There are several disadvantages:

- If your course content changes frequently, Google might index out-of-date information for your courses.
- Your students and teachers might not want their names and materials indexed and available to the public.

- If Google indexes all of your guest-enabled courses, you have less control over what information about your site appears in Google. Everything on the pages that the Googlebot searches is used in indexing your site. There might be items on those pages that don't accurately represent your site. For example, a negative forum posting or an off-topic discussion could become associated with your site. Also, if the focus or structure of your Moodle site changes, it may take awhile before all the Google references to all those pages are corrected.

If you want strict control over what information appears in Google about your site, then set opentogoogle to No. Put only the information that you want to appear in Google on the Front Page of your site, and do not allow teachers or students to modify anything on the Front Page. This way, Google will index only your Front Page. You should also request anyone who links to your site to link only to the Front Page (for example, "Please link only to http//www.moodle.williamrice.com, not directly to a course page.") Google and other search engines use links to your site to calculate your ranking. If all those links point to the same page, you can better control your site's public image. By setting opentogoogle to No, and requesting that people link only to the Front Page, you are trading away some of your search engine presence in exchange for greater control of your site's public image.

For the ultimate in control of what information about your site is indexed, consider this plan: set forcelogin to Yes to keep search engine robots out of Moodle completely. Set opentogoogle to No to prevent Google from crawling your guest courses. Set autologinguests to No to eliminate the possibility that any other search engine's robots crawl your guest courses. Now you've locked out all but registered users.

Put Moodle into a subdirectory of your site. Link to Moodle from the index page at the root of your site. In my case, I would put Moodle into moodle.williamrice.com/moodle/ and link to it from moodle.williamrice.com/index.htm. Then, use index.htm as an introduction to your site. Ensure that index.htm contains exactly the kind of information you want the public to know about your site, and optimize it for the best search engine placement.

enablerssfeeds

An **RSS** feed is when a website supplies selected content to the rest of the world. It stands for **Really Simple Syndication**. You may have seen web pages that have a section where news from a major news source appears. For example, my personal site has RSS feeds from Web Developer News and BBC: Technology in the left column:

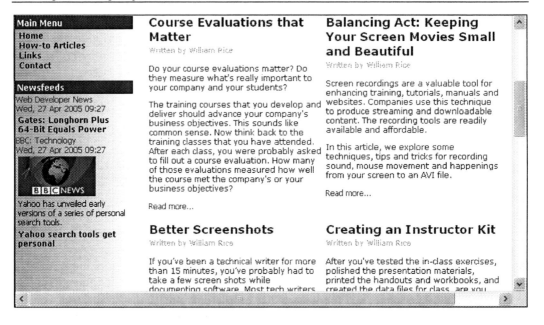

Those RSS feeds are updated periodically.

You can also enable RSS feeds for your Moodle site. This variable enables and disables the feeds site-wide. Then, for each module you enable RSS feeds individually. For example, your Moodle site can feed, or syndicate, the latest forum entries by enabling RSS feeds here and in the Forums module (under Administration | Configuration | Modules | Forum Settings). Remember that you're not using RSS to announce the latest content changes inside your Moodle site. You're using it to announce those changes to the rest of the world.

RSS feeds can be read by most popular email clients, such as **Outlook**, **Thunderbird**, and **Netscape Mail**. This is probably how your students will receive the RSS feeds from your learning site. In the following example, I've subscribed to http://www.moodle.org's RSS feed. Notice how each individual feed shows up as an email.

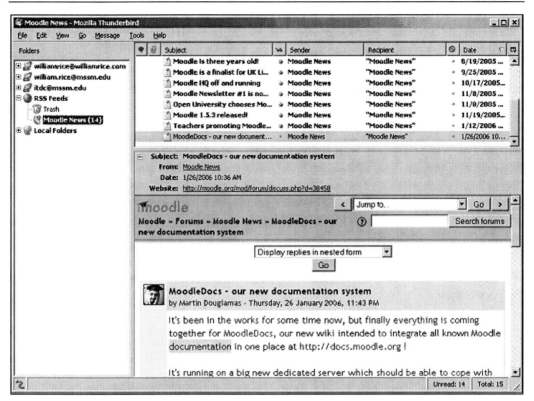

The site administrator must use this setting to enable RSS feeds. The administrator can choose to allow only the administrator to create RSS feeds, or to allow teachers to create RSS feeds. Allowing teachers to create RSS feeds enables them to add RSS to the courses they teach. For example, a teacher could add RSS to a course forum. Assuming the students use their email program to get RSS feeds, the students would then see a new feed item when the forum is updated. This is a good way for the teacher to stay in touch with the students.

digestmailtime

This is the time that email digests get sent to users who have subscribed to digests. It is the time on the server, so if your server is located in a different time zone than you or your students, consider the time difference when setting this.

Installation Step 8: Upgrading the Database and Setting Up Tables

After stepping through a few more screens, `install.php` upgrades the Moodle database and creates more tables. You don't need to do anything during this part of the installation except click to see the next screen. The installation script tells you when this is complete.

Installation Step 9: Site Settings

After creating the database tables, the installation script displays the Site settings page. The values you enter on this page affect Moodle's Front Page. Of course, you want to enter them correctly the first time. However, after Moodle is installed, you can return to this page at any time to change these variables.

The screenshot below shows the top of the Site settings page for my demonstration site. Notice the breadcrumbs line at the top shows that I'm on the site whose short name is wildskills, and that to get to this page I've selected Administration, then Configuration, and then Site settings:

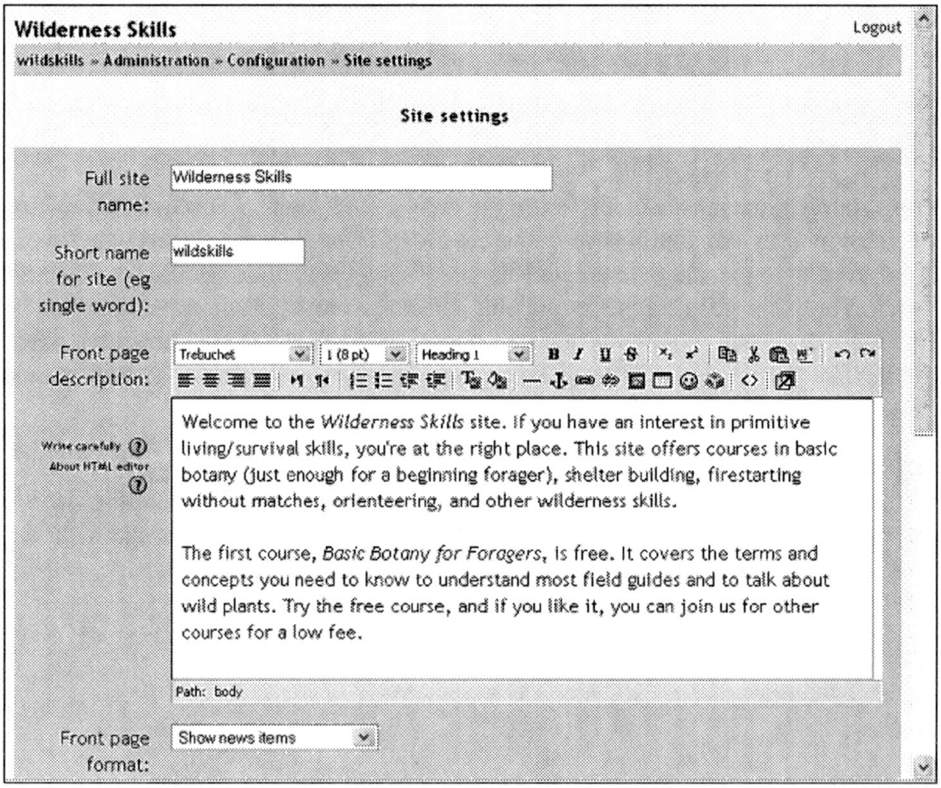

Let's examine how each of the Site settings influences the Front Page and the user experience.

Full Site Name

The full site name appears at the top of the Front Page, in the browser's title bar, and also on the page tab in Netscape or Firefox:

> **Wilderness Skills - Mozilla Firefox**
> File Edit View Go Bookmarks Tools Help
> http://moodle.williamrice.com/
> Wilderness Skills   Using Moodle: Recent A
>
> **Wilderness Skills**

The full site name also appears in the metadata for the Front Page. Here are the first few lines of HTML code from my Front Page. The line containing the full site name is in bold:

```
<html dir="ltr">
<head>
<meta http-equiv="content-type" content="text/html; charset=iso-8859-
1" />
<style type="text/css">@import
url(http://moodle.williamrice.com/lib/editor/htmlarea.css);</style>
<meta name="description" content="
Welcome to the Wilderness Skills site. If you have an interest in
primitive living/survival skills, you're at the right place. This
site offers courses in basic botany (just enough for a beginning
forager), shelter building, firestarting without matches,
orienteering, and other wilderness skills. The first course, Basic
Botany for Foragers, is free. It covers the terms and concepts you
need to know to understand most field guides and to talk about wild
plants. Try the free course, and if you like it, you can join us for
other courses for a low fee.">

<title>Wilderness Skills</title>
<meta name="keywords" content="moodle, Wilderness Skills " />
```

Short Name for Site

Once a user enters your Moodle site, a navigation line is displayed at the top of each page. This shows the user where he or she is in the site. The first item in this navigation line, or breadcrumb trail, is the short site name:

Front Page Description

This description appears in the left or right column of your site's Front Page. If you require visitors to register and log in before seeing the Front Page (see *forcelogin* under *Installation Step 7d: Specify Site Variables*), remember that visitors will see this information after they have logged in. In that case, the Front Page description can't be used to sell your site. Instead, it can instruct students on how to get started with your site. For example, "Take the Introduction course to learn how to use this site..."

If your Front Page is visible to all visitors, then you can use this description to sell your site, tempt visitors to take a sample course, tell them what's inside, etc.

Remember that the Front Page description always appears in the left or right column of the Front Page. It does not appear in the center column. If you want your site description (e.g. Welcome to the....) top and center, you'll need to include a topic section (covered next), which always appears in the center of your Front Page. You would make your site description the first topic. In this case, you turn the Front Page Description off.

Also, this description appears in the metadata of the first page:

```
<html dir="ltr">
<head>
<meta http-equiv="content-type" content="text/html; charset=iso-8859-
1" />
<style type="text/css">@import
url(http://moodle.williamrice.com/lib/editor/htmlarea.css);</style>
<meta name="description" content="
Welcome to the Wilderness Skills site. If you have an interest in
primitive living/survival skills, you're at the right place. This
site offers courses in basic botany (just enough for a beginning
forager), shelter building, firestarting without matches,
orienteering, and other wilderness skills. The first course, Basic
Botany for Foragers, is free. It covers the terms and concepts you
need to know to understand most field guides and to talk about wild
plants. Try the free course, and if you like it, you can join us for
other courses for a low fee.">

<title>Wilderness Skills</title>
<meta name="keywords" content="moodle, Wilderness Skills " />
```

The implication here is that even if you plan to use a Topic section to put your site description top and center, instead of using the Front Page Description in a column on the left or right side, you should type your site description into this field. Even though you've turned off the Front Page Description, it will still show up in the metadata, which can be helpful for optimizing search engine results.

Front Page Format

This setting determines whether the center column of the Front Page shows news items, a list of courses, or a list of course categories. Each setting has its unique advantages.

Show News items

This setting is useful if the content of your site changes frequently, and you want to keep visitors informed. If one of the primary purposes of your Front Page is serving repeat customers, showing news items on the Front Page is a good idea.

The downside is that the list of course categories is now relegated to a side column. If you want the course categories, or courses themselves, to be displayed more prominently, you'll need to use Show a list of categories or Show a list of courses.

Show a List of Categories

This setting is useful if you want to make it easy for your students to find and select a course. It puts the course categories in the center of the Front Page. The drawback is that you no longer have a news section at the center and top for your repeat visitors.

Front page
format: [Show a list of courses ▾]

Wilderness Skills

Login
[English (en_us) ▾]

Main menu

📄 About Wilderness Skills
📄 How to Use this Site
📄 Enroll for a Course

Desert Plants Course Added

A new course has been added to our Wild Plants section. After taking our free course, *Basic Botany for Foragers*, you're ready to learn about the plants found in some of the harshest places on Earth.

Course categories

Free Courses	1
Wild Plants	3
Tracking and Animal	2

Welcome to the *Wilderness Skills* site. If you have an interest in primitive living/survival skills, you're at the right place. This site offers courses in basic botany (just enough for a beginning forager), shelter building, firestarting without matches, orienteering, and other wilderness skills.

I've added a topic section to the Front Page (this is covered next). The topic section gave me an area where I can add course resources. To this topic section, I added a label. The label consists of the Desert Plants Course Added notice that you see in the screenshot. The label is not as convenient to manage as a news area. However, this method does enable me to get the course categories on the Front Page, while still posting an announcement center top.

Notice that in the previous screenshot, for Show news items, I chose to keep the course category listing in the left column. Now that I'm showing course categories in the center, the list of categories in the left-hand block became superfluous. Later, we'll cover how to turn blocks off and on for the Front Page.

Show a List of Courses

Notice also that I've added a Main menu in the left column, with links to detailed information about the site, how to use it, and the enrollment/payment page. The welcome message in the right column and the links to detailed information about the site in the left column serves my new visitors. The label (announcement), Desert Plants Course Added and course options Available Courses in the center serve my existing customers.

Front page
format: Show a list of courses ▼

Wilderness Skills

Login
English (en_us) ▼

Main menu

📄 About Wilderness Skills
📄 How to Use this Site
📄 Enroll for a Course

Desert Plants Course Added

A new course has been added to our Wild Plants section. After taking our free course, *Basic Botany for Foragers*, you're ready to learn about the plants found in some of the harshest places on Earth.

Available Courses

Free Courses

FREE COURSE: Basic Botany for Foragers 🖉 ❶

Wild Plants

A Walk on the Beach ❶

By the Water's Edge ❶

Desert Plants ❶

Tracking and Animal Observation

Tracking Basics ❶

Welcome to the *Wilderness Skills* site. If you have an interest in primitive living/survival skills, you're at the right place. This site offers courses in basic botany (just enough for a beginning forager), shelter building, firestarting without matches, orienteering, and other wilderness skills.

The first course, *Basic Botany for Foragers*, is free. It covers the terms and concepts you need to know to understand most field guides and to talk about wild plants. Try the free course, and if you

---

This setting makes it as easy as possible for students to find the course they're looking for. It can also be a powerful marketing tool. Notice the ❶ icon next to each course. Clicking this gives the visitor a description of the course (later in the section on creating courses, you'll see how to enter a course description). If you want to encourage visitors to do this, you could insert another label between the announcement Desert Plants Course Added and the Available Courses section, saying something like, "For a short description of each course, click on the ❶ next to it."

The drawback to using Show a list of courses is that the course list can get very long. You must decide how much tolerance your visitors are likely to have for scrolling and browsing through a long list of courses.

Configuration Choices after Installation

You won't be prompted for these configuration choices, but after installation you should look at these settings. You may want to make some choices immediately after installation, and others you may want to delay. All of these settings can be changed later.

Filters

You'll find the Filters settings under Administration | Configuration | Filters. Filters go through all the text that you enter in your courses, and process this text. For the most part, Filters create an automatic link whenever a glossary term or learning resource is mentioned on your site. They also handle special mathematical notation. Read the descriptions below for detailed information about what filters can do for your site.

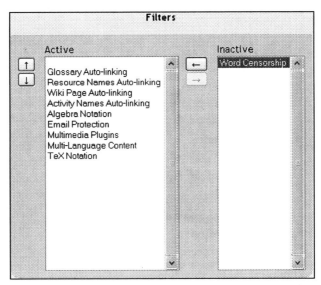

Auto-Linking Filters

The Auto-linking filters search the text on your site, and automatically link to items when they find an item mentioned in the text. For example, Glossary Auto-linking looks for terms that are in any glossary, and when it finds them links the term to the glossary entry. The term is highlighted, and when a user clicks it, the user is taken to the glossary.

Resource Names Auto-linking searches course text for the names of course resources. When it finds the name of a resource, it links the name to the resource. This means whenever a student sees the name of a document, web page, or other course resource, the student can just click on the name and be taken to the resource. Activity Names Auto-linking works the same way for course activities. Wiki Page Auto-linking creates a link to a Wiki page whenever the page is mentioned on the site.

Math Filters

Algebra Notation and TeX Notation search the text for special characters used to describe mathematical formulas. For example, if you enter @@cosh(x,2)@@ the Algebra Notation filter will display it as:

$$\cosh^2{(x)}$$

If you enter $$ \Bigsum_{i=\1}^{n-\1}$$, the TeX Notation filter will display it as:

$$\sum_{i=1}^{n-1}$$

Algebra Notation and TeX Notation are standard markup languages. The http://www.moodle.org site contains more information about Algebra Notation. For more information about TeX, see the TeX Users Group at tug.org. TeX is more mature and complete than Algebra Notation. If you plan on writing more complex equations, I suggest making the TeX Notation filter active and leaving the Algebra Notation filter inactive.

Email Protection Filter

Activating this filter makes email addresses on the site unreadable to search engines, while keeping them 'human-readable'. If you set opentogoogle to No, or require users to log in, then you probably don't need to worry about search engines automatically picking up your students' email addresses. If your site is open to search engines and anonymous users, then you might want to use this filter to protect the users' email addresses.

Multimedia Plugins

If you leave this filter inactive, then multimedia content will usually play in a separate window. For example, without this filter, when a user clicks on a video, that video might open and play in a separate **Windows Media Player** or **RealPlayer** window. By activating this filter, you embed multimedia so that it plays on the page in which it was linked.

Multi-Language Content

In the Variables screen, you used the variable langlist to determine which languages, if any, users can select. When a user selects one of these languages, only the Moodle interface is translated. The course content remains in whatever language you created it. If you want your site to be truly **multi-lingual**, you can also create course content in several languages. Activating the Multi-Language Content filter will then cause the course material to be displayed in the selected language.

To create course content in multiple languages, you must enclose text written in each language in a <span> tag, like this:

```
<span lang="en">Basic Botany</span>
<span lang="es">Botánica Básica</span>
```

This requires that you write course material in HTML. This can be done for headings, course descriptions, course material, and any other HTML document that Moodle displays.

Filter Uploaded files

Setting this to Yes applies the activated filters to files that teachers and students upload to Moodle. When set to No, Moodle's filters apply only to content created in Moodle.

Backup

You'll find the backup settings under Administration | Configuration | Backup. Most of these settings enable you to choose the type of data that gets backed up. You also choose on which days of the week the backup will automatically run. The backup is activated by the cron job routine (see *Installation Step 6: Setting up the Cron Job*).

The backups are stored in compressed, or ZIP format. In the Variables page, you indicated if your hosting service has a zip program or if Moodle should use its own, built-in zip program (see *zip and unzip* under *Installation Step 7d: Specify Site Variables*). If you activate automatic backups, and Moodle must use its built-in zip program during the backups, you might see backup failures caused by lack of memory. If you plan on using the backup feature for more than a handful of courses, ensure that your hosting service offers a zip program on its servers.

Authentication

Authentication and login are different. Authentication is what happens when a new user signs up for your site, and creates a new Moodle account. Login is when an authenticated user logs into Moodle.

Moodle offers a variety of ways to authenticate users. You'll find them under Administration | Users | Authentication options. Each of the options is explained on that page. This subsection will fill in a few key blanks left by Moodle's explanations.

When you authenticate users with an external database (MySQL, Oracle, etc.), Moodle copies over the username and password from the external database into Moodle's internal database. From then on, when the user logs into Moodle, it uses Moodle's internal database to check the username and password. There is no live link between the external database and Moodle's user database. This means that if the user changes his or her username and password in the external database, the username and password in Moodle is not changed.

When you authenticate users with a server (LDAP, IMAP, etc.), Moodle checks the username and password against that server every time the user logs in. If the user changes his or her password on the server, the user will have that new password in Moodle.

If you authenticate against an external database or an LDAP server, you can have Moodle bring over user information from the database or server. This user information is copied into Moodle at the time of authentication. For example, Moodle can copy over the user's first name, last name, and email address. Once it's copied into Moodle, it is no longer synchronized with the external database.

Enrolment Choices

Enrolment is different from authentication. In authentication, you confirm a user's membership to your site. In enrolment, you grant or confirm a user's access to a course. You have several options for managing student enrolment. They are found under Administration | Users | Enrolments.

External Database

You can use an external database to control student enrolment. In this case, Moodle looks in the designated database and determines if the student is enrolled. As of version 1.4, Moodle will not write back to the external database. All changes in the external database are made by another program.

In addition to using the external database, you can also allow Moodle's normal enrolment routine. Checking enrol_allowinternal enables this feature. If you enable internal enrolment in addition the external database, Moodle checks two databases when a student tries to enter a course: the external one, and its internal one.

In the External Database screen, you designate which field in Moodle corresponds to the course name field in the external database. In the example overleaf, you can see the Edit course settings for the Basic Botany course. I've given this course an ID number of 0001. This course ID number will correspond to the same ID number in the external database. To match the field ID number from course settings against the external database, I need to enter the field name for ID number in enrol_localcoursefield.

The temptation is to type ID number into enrol_localcoursefield, since ID number is what you see in the Edit Course Settings screen. Surely that is the field name, right? Well, no. Take look at the Moodle database, in the md1_course table, and you'll see the real name of this field is idnumber:

Similarly, we would look up the field name for the student's ID number, and enter that into enrol_localuserfield.

Flat File

The flat file method of student enrolment causes Moodle to read in a text file, or "flat file," and use that as the source for enrolment information. The flat file has this format:

```
operation, role, ID number of user, ID number of course
```

where:

- `operation` is add or del.
- `role` is student, teacher, or teacheredit.
- `ID number of user` is the field idnumber from the database table md1_user.

ID number of course is the field idnumber from the database table md1_course.

Moodle periodically reads in this file, and modifies its enrolment data according to what the file says. For example, the line

```
add, student, 0005, WP102
```

will add the student with the ID number of 0005 to the course with the ID number of WP102.

Place this file in a directory that is accessible to your web server. For example, you can put it inside the data directory.

Internal Enrolment

This is the default form of enrolment. When this is selected, there are two ways to enroll a student in a course:

- A teacher or administrator can enroll the student. From within the course, the teacher selects Students and is taken to the Enroll students screen.
- The prospective student is supplied with an **enrolment key**. Using this key, the student can enroll in the course.

Paypal

The Paypal option enables you to set up paid access to the site, or to individual courses. When you select this option, if you enter a value of zero into enrol_cost, students can access the site for free. If you enter a non-zero amount, students must pay to access the site.

Selecting this option puts an enrol_cost field into the Edit Course Settings screen Wildskills | Administration | Users | Enrolments of every course. Again, entering a non-zero amount into this field requires students to pay to access the course.

The Paypal payment screen displays a notice that this course requires a payment for entry. It also contains a button labeled Send payment via Paypal. You can modify this screen by modifying the source file at enrol/paypal/enrol.php.

Summary

This chapter tells you how to make changes to the Variables page. The values you enter on this page affect the behavior of the entire site. The values you enter on the Site settings page affect Moodle's Front Page.

It covers the creation of the database, which is also very important. You need to know the correct amount of disk space and the bandwidth required for the software. It also covers the ways of authenticating Moodle users and how your choice affects the operation of your site.

It also helps you to make the right configuration choices during and after the installation process. You can edit the choices, if you have already made any. The configuration choices that are made during the installation process affect the student and teacher experience in Moodle.

Once you have completed the installation of Moodle, you can continue with the next chapter, *Creating Categories and Courses*. It will help you understand how to create course structures and settings and change them as needed.

3
Creating Categories and Courses

This chapter's focus is on helping you create different categories and courses. While someone else may have installed Moodle and made these choices for you, you can always go back and change them.

The following sections will help you to create and organize course categories. It will also tell you how to put a course into several categories.

Using Course Categories and the User Experience

Every Moodle course belongs to one course category. When a student selects a course, the student must first select a category. In the next example, the student selected the Tracking and Animal Observation category from the Front Page, and is selecting a course from that category:

Notice that even though the student is looking at the Tracking and Animal Observation category, a drop-down list of Course categories enables the student to see the other categories. Typical of Moodle, this enables the student to jump to another part of the site without having to return to the Front Page.

Categories are a site-wide way to organize your courses. You can also create subcategories. The categories or subcategories become an online course catalog. Organize them in the same intuitive way as you would a printed course catalog.

Creating Course Categories

You create course categories in the Administration | Course categories screen. After logging in as an administrator, the fastest way to reach this screen is selecting Courses from the Administration block.

In the resulting screen, you create new categories and courses. You also arrange the order in which the categories are displayed:

Organizing Course Categories

To move a course category up or down in the list, click the ↑ or ↓ in the Edit column. To hide a course category while you're working on it, click ☀. The eye will then close, indicating the category is hidden from users. To delete a category, select ✗.

You can use subcategories in Moodle. For example, suppose I want to categorize the Wild Plants courses by habitat. In the following page, you can see that I've added two new categories, Woodlands and Jungle. I've hidden these categories because I'm still working on them. I moved Woodlands to the Wild Plants category, making Woodlands a subcategory. I am in the process of making Jungle a subcategory of Wild Plants:

Course categories	Courses	Edit	Move category to:
Free Courses	1	✗ ☀ ↓	Top
Wild Plants	3	✗ ☀ ↑ ↓	Top
Woodlands	0	✗ ⌣	Wild Plants
Tracking and Animal Observation	2	✗ ☀ ↑ ↓	Top
Shelter and Fire	2	✗ ☀ ↑ ↓	Top
Jungle	0	✗ ⌣ ↑	Top
			Top
			Free Courses
			Wild Plants
		Add a new course	Wild Plants / Woodlands
			Tracking and Animal Observation
			Shelter and Fire

Putting a Course into Several Categories

One of Moodle's limitations is that you can put a course into only one category. In some situations, you might want to put the same course into several categories. You have several options:

- You can forego the use of categories, and use direct links to the courses. In Chapter 4, you'll see how to add labels and links to the Front Page. You can use labels as your category names, and put the links below the labels.

- You can create the course in one category, duplicate it, and upload the copy into another category. This has the disadvantage of requiring you to manage two separate courses. Students might also become confused about which iteration of the course they enrolled in.

- You can create the course in one category, and then create an identically named course in the second category. However, you will put only one thing into the second course: a **JavaScript** that automatically forwards the user to the real course.

You can search the Web for a free JavaScript to use, or here is one from http://javascriptkit.com/ that you can add to the course as a label:

```
<form name="redirect">
<center>
<font face="Arial"><b>You will be redirected to the script in<br><br>
<form>
<input type="text" size="3" name="redirect2">
</form>
seconds</b></font>
</center>

<script>
<!--

/*
Count down then redirect script
By JavaScript Kit (http://javascriptkit.com)
Over 400+ free scripts here!
*/

//change below target URL to your own
var targetURL="http://javascriptkit.com"
//change the second to start counting down from
var countdownfrom=10

var currentsecond=document.redirect.redirect2.value=countdownfrom+1
function countredirect(){
if (currentsecond!=1){
currentsecond-=1
document.redirect.redirect2.value=currentsecond
}
else{
window.location=targetURL
return
}
setTimeout("countredirect()",1000)
}

countredirect()
//-->
</script>
```

Creating Courses

Don't worry if you mistakenly put a course into the wrong category. In the next section, *The Course Settings Page*, you can change the category. You can also do this from the administration screen:

1. Select Administration | Course categories.
2. Select the category that currently holds the course.
3. Click the checkbox next to the course whose category you want to change.
4. From the drop-down list, select the new category for the course.

The Course Settings Page

When you create a course, you must fill out fields on the Course Settings page. Many of these fields are self-explanatory. Some of them, especially Format and Group mode, have a profound effect on the user experience. You can always return to this page and change the course settings. The course, and its structure, will be updated with the new settings as soon as you save them.

The page itself does a good job of explaining the purpose of each setting. However, the directions do not tell you the implications of the choices you make on this page. In the following, I've added some commentary to help you determine how your choices will affect the operation of your site, and information to help you decide upon the right choices for your needs.

Category

If you selected a course category and then created the course, you'll see the category displayed in this field. You can use the drop-down list to change the category at any time. The list shows both visible and hidden categories.

As your site grows and you add categories, you may want to reorganize your site. However, if a student logs in while you are in the middle of creating categories and moving courses, he or she might be confused. It would be best if you can make the reorganization as quickly as possible—ideally, instantaneously.

You can speed the reorganization time by hiding your categories as you create them. This lets you take your time while thinking about what categories to use. Then, move the courses into the categories. Each course will disappear until you finally reveal the new categories.

Full Name and Short Name

The full name of the course appears at the top of the page when viewing the course, and also in course listings. The short name appears in the breadcrumb trail, at the top of the page. In this example, the full name is Basic Botany for Foragers and the short name is Wild Plants 1:

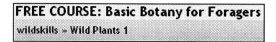

FREE COURSE: Basic Botany for Foragers
wildskills » Wild Plants 1

The full name also appears in the page's title and metadata, which influences its search engine rankings. Here's the HTML code from the example above:

```
<title>Course: FREE COURSE: Basic Botany for Foragers</title>
<meta name="keywords" content="moodle, Course: FREE COURSE: Basic
Botany for Foragers " />
```

Notice the full course name in the <title> and <meta> tags. Many search engines give a lot of weight to the title and keywords tags. Choose your course title with this in mind.

ID Number

The section dealing with the variable langlist in Chapter 2 talks about using an external database for enrolment information. The ID number that you enter into this field must match the ID number of the course in the External Database. If you're not using an external database for enrolment information, you can leave this field blank.

Summary

The Summary is displayed when a reader clicks on the info icon, and when the course appears in a list:

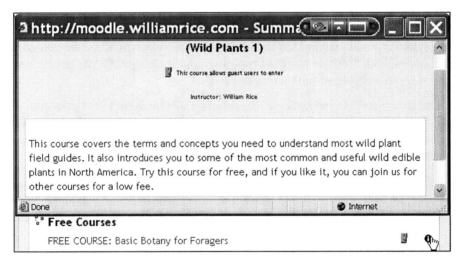

Wilderness Skills: Courses

wildskills » Course categories » Free Courses   [   ] [Search courses]

Course categories: [Free Courses   ▾]

FREE COURSE: Basic Botany for Foragers

Instructor: William Rice

This course covers the terms and concepts you need to understand most wild plant field guides. It also introduces you to some of the most common and useful wild edible plants in North America. Try this course for free, and if you like it, you can join us for other courses for a low fee.

If you allow visitors to see your Front Page without logging in, then they will probably read your course summaries before enrolling. Consider the Summary to be a course's resume. Your course summaries need to be informative and work as a sales tool. They should offer enough information to help your visitors decide if they want to enroll, and should describe the courses in their best light.

Format

You can select three formats for a course:

- Topics
- Weekly (this is the default format for a new course)
- Social

The subsections below explain how each format affects the user experience.

Topics Format

The Topics format is the most intuitive format to use for a course. Because it displays each part of the course as a numbered topic, this format encourages most students to proceed through the course sequentially. However, it does not enforce this sequence, so students are free to jump ahead and behind in the course.

Welcome

Have you ever picked up a wild plants field guide, read a plant's description, and felt confused by all those specialized botanical terms? It's as if they expect you to have a degree in botany before reading the book. Or have you ever tried to memorize a few wild edible plants just by reading their descriptions over and over, but gave up trying to memorize them by brute force?

If so, this course is for you.

Welcome to *Basic Botany for Foragers*. This course introduces you to foraging. Foraging is identifying, gathering, and using wild plants for food, medicine, and tools.

Before continuing, it is very important that you read and understand the following warning: **Eat only those plants you can positively identify and that you know are safe to eat. Identify and collect wild plants only under the guidance of an experienced forager. This course is an excellent preparation for learning to identify plants under the guidance of an expert, but is not a substitute. You should learn under someone qualified and experienced in the collection of wild plants in your area. Common sense dictates that if you have any doubt as to a plant's safety, don't eat it.**

To learn more about this course, select *Course Goals and Outline* below. To meet your fellow foragers, join the *Course Discussion*. To jump into the course, just select a lesson.

Course Goals and Outline

Course Discussion

1 Types of Plants

Identifying the basic types of plants: woody, herbaceous, and succulents.

2 Life Cycles of Plants

Like all living things, plants have a life cycle. This lesson covers the different types of life cycles found in the plant world.

3 Leaves

Leaves are one of the most important identifying features of a plant. This section covers many of the terms used in field guides and botany texts.

4 Flowers

Along with leaves, flowers are the most important identifying feature. This section covers flower parts and terminology used to describe

Every course has a Topic 0. In this example, Topic 0 includes the Welcome message, Course Goals and Outline, and the Course Discussion board. I put this introductory information under Topic 0 so that Topics 1 through 7 could be reserved for lessons. This further reinforces the sequential feel of the course.

Weekly Format

The Weekly format appears almost identical to the Topics format, except that it displays dates for each topic. As of this writing, Moodle does not automatically enforce these dates. That is, Moodle does not turn on and off weekly sections on the appropriate dates. The site administrator or teacher must do that. Alternatively, you can just allow students to access the weeks in any order.

Weekly outline

Welcome

Have you ever picked up a wild plants field guide, read a plant's description, and felt confused by all those specialized botanical terms? It's as if they expect you to have a degree in botany before reading the book. Or have you ever tried to memorize a few wild edible plants just by reading their descriptions over and over, but gave up trying to memorize them by brute force?

If so, this course is for you.

Welcome to *Basic Botany for Foragers*. This course introduces you to foraging. Foraging is identifying, gathering, and using wild plants for food, medicine, and tools.

Before continuing, it is very important that you read and understand the following warning: **Eat only those plants you can positively identify and that you know are safe to eat. Identify and collect wild plants only under the guidance of an experienced forager. This course is an excellent preparation for learning to identify plants under the guidance of an expert, but is not a substitute. You should learn under someone qualified and experienced in the collection of wild plants in your area. Common sense dictates that if you have any doubt as to a plant's safety, don't eat it.**

To learn more about this course, select *Course Goals and Outline* below. To meet your fellow foragers, join the *Course Discussion*. To jump into the course, just select a lesson.

📖 Course Goals and Outline
🗫 Course Discussion

1   May 3 - May 9 □

Types of Plants

Identifying the basic types of plants: woody, herbaceous, and succulents.

2   May 10 - May 16 (Not available) □

3   May 17 - May 23 (Not available) □

4   May 24 - May 30 (Not available) □

In the example shown here, we've selected the Weekly format, and then hidden each of the future weeks (we'll cover hiding and revealing course weeks/topics later). The only week showing is the current one. We also chose to allow hidden weeks to appear in collapsed form instead of making them disappear completely. Students can access this week, and see how many weeks remain in the course. In this arrangement, each week the site administrator or teacher will need to reveal or "unhide" that week's topic.

We could also have completely hidden the future weeks, and then put a list of the weeks in the Welcome message. It would look like the example below. Either way the result is the same: the current and past weeks are available, and students can immediately see how many weeks remain.

Welcome

Have you ever picked up a wild plants field guide, read a plant's description, and felt confused by all those specialized botanical terms? It's as if they expect you to have a degree in botany before reading the book. Or have you ever tried to memorize a few wild edible plants just by reading their descriptions over and over, but gave up trying to memorize them by brute force?

If so, this course is for you.

Welcome to *Basic Botany for Foragers*. This course introduces you to foraging. Foraging is identifying, gathering, and using wild plants for food, medicine, and tools.

Before continuing, it is very important that you read and understand the following warning: **Eat only those plants you can positively identify and that you know are safe to eat. Identify and collect wild plants only under the guidance of an experienced forager. This course is an excellent preparation for learning to identify plants under the guidance of an expert, but is not a substitute. You should learn under someone qualified and experienced in the collection of wild plants in your area. Common sense dictates that if you have any doubt as to a plant's safety, don't eat it.**

To learn more about this course, select *Course Goals and Outline* below. To meet your fellow foragers, join the *Course Discussion*. To jump into the course, just select a lesson.

<>

Schedule for *Basic Botany for Foragers*

Week	Lesson	Description
1: May 3-9	Types of Plants	Identifying the basic types of plants: woody, herbaceous, and succulents.
2: May 10-16	Life Cycles of Plants	Like all living things, plants have a life cycle. This lesson covers the different types of life cycles found in the plant world.
3: May 17-23	Leaves	Leaves are one of the most important identifying features of a plant. This section covers many of the terms used in field guides and botany texts.
4: May 24-30	Flowers	Along with leaves, flowers are the most important identifying feature. This section covers flower parts and terminology used to describe flowers.
5: May 31-June 6	Roots	During winter and spring, when leaves and flowers are absent or undeveloped, a plant's roots can be an important identifying feature.

Social Format

The Social course format turns the entire course into one discussion forum. Discussion topics are displayed on the course's Home Page, as you see in the screenshot given. Replies to a topic are added and read by clicking on Discuss this topic.

One of the settings available for forums enables you to prevent students from creating new topics, so that they can only post replies to existing topics (later, we will cover the settings that are available in a forum). Only the administrator or teacher can create new topics, which appear on the course's Home Page. Students then discuss these topics by adding replies to them. This enables you to better control the discussion, and to prevent the creation of so many topics that the course's Home Page becomes too long.

The Social format is very different from a traditional, sequential course. It lacks the organization and ability to add activities and resources that you find in this Topic and Weekly formats. However, because the Social format turns the entire course into a discussion forum, it offers you the chance to put a discussion forum right into the course listings. In this example, we created a course called Discussion, selected the Social course format, and put it into the Free Courses category. Now it appears in the course listing on the Front Page:

Notice the block listing course categories in the left column. If you choose to display this block, students can always quickly get to the list of courses. Because Wilderness Skills Discussions is a course, this means that students can always get to the site-wide forum quickly and conveniently.

Instead of using a Social course for the site-wide forum, we could have just added a discussion forum to the site's Front Page, like this:

Notice Wilderness Skills Discussions just beneath the news item, near the top. It's not as prominent as when the site-wide forum was a course. Also, because it doesn't appear in the Free Courses category, it's not immediately apparent that the forum is free and open to all. Finally, if a student is in a course and wants to get to this forum, the student must navigate back to the Front Page, which is less convenient than clicking on the ever-present Courses in the left column. For this site, making Wilderness Skills Discussions into a Social course and putting it into the Free Courses category is the better option.

Course Start Date

For a Weekly course, this field sets the starting date shown. It has no effect on the display of Topic or Social courses. Students can enter a course as soon as you display it; the course start date does not shut off or hide a course until the start date. This field's only other effect is that logs for course activity begin on this date.

Enrolment Period

This field specifies the maximum length of time a user can be enrolled in the course.
After the time is up, the student is automatically unenrolled.

> The maximum time of enrollment is one year.

If you leave this set to Unlimited, you must manually unenrol students from this course.
When you learn about using Discussions (or Forums) in your courses, you'll learn that
one of the uses for a Forum is to send a mass email to everyone enrolled in a course. You
do this by selecting a setting that forces everyone enrolled in a course to be subscribed to
the forum, and then posting the message to the forum. The message will be broadcast to
everyone in the course. Be aware that if you leave all students enrolled permanently,
students who are no longer participating in the course will still get these announcements.

Number of Weeks/Topics

This specifies the number of weeks or topics (sections) in a course.

Adding and Removing Sections

If you want to add weeks or topics to a course, just use this pull-down menu to select the
greater number of sections. Additional sections will be added. If you select fewer sections
than you have now, sections will be deleted. However, if there is content in the deleted
sections, it is not lost. Just select the greater number of sections again, and when the
deleted sections are restored, so is their content.

Using Extra, Hidden Sections

Remember that you can hide sections. If you choose to make hidden sections completely
invisible to students (that setting is covered under the section Hidden Sections), then
there is no real disadvantage to having more sections than you're using. You can keep a
section that you're working on hidden, and then reveal it when you're finished. If you
want to modify an existing section, you can create a hidden duplicate of the section, work
on it, and with a few clicks in a few seconds, hide the old section and reveal the new one.

You can move resources between sections in a course. This makes a hidden section a
convenient place to hold resources that you might want to use later, or that you want to
archive. For example, if you find a site on the Web that you might want to use in your
course later, but you're not sure, you can create a link to the site in a hidden section. If
you eventually decide you want to use the site, you can just move that link from the
hidden section to one of the sections in use.

Using Group Mode

Group mode applies to activities in this course. Each course can have no or several groups. When set to No groups, all students in the course are considered to be in one big group. When set to Separate groups, all of the students in the same group can see each other's work. However, students in different groups, even though they are in the same course, cannot see work from another group. That is, the work done by different groups is kept separate. When set to Visible groups, students are divided into groups but can still see work from other groups. That is, the work done by one group's students is visible to the other groups' students.

Running Separate Groups Through a Course, versus Having Separate Courses

Using Separate groups enables you to reuse a course for many groups, while giving the impression to each group that the course is theirs alone. However, this doesn't work well for a Weekly format course, where the weeks are dated. If you start each group on a different date, the weekly dates will become incorrect.

If you're running a Topics format course, you can easily reuse the course by separating your students into groups and running each group individually. Later, you'll see how to assign teachers to a course. You can also assign a teacher to a group, so that teacher can see only his or her students.

If you run several groups through a course, and those groups are at different points in the course, be aware that the teacher cannot regulate the flow of students through the course by turning topics off and on. That is, you cannot reveal just Topic 1 until the group has finished it, and then reveal Topic 2 until the group has worked through it, and then Topic 3 and so on. This would be one way of enforcing the order of the course for a single group. However, if you tried this while running several groups who were at different points in the course, you'd be turning off topics that some groups need.

If you really must enforce the order of topics by revealing them one at a time, create a copy of the course for each group. Later, we'll cover duplicating courses.

Force Group Mode

Normally, the course's Group mode can be overridden for each activity. When the course creator adds an activity, the creator can choose a different Group mode than the default set for the course. However, when Force is set to Yes, all activities have the same Group mode as the course.

Availability

While you're working on a course, you may want to set this to This course is not available to students. This will completely hide your course from students' view.

Teachers and administrators can still see the course, so you can collaborate on the course content with them.

Use Enrollment Keys to Regulate Access

If you enter an Enrollment key, each student must enter the key the first time he or she enters the course. Once a student has given the key and entered the course, the student can access the course without the key.

If you change the key, students who have already accessed the course under the old key can continue to do so. However, new students will need to enter the new key the first time they enter the course.

You usually supply the Enrollment key using something other than Moodle. For example, if you're charging for courses, you can put the Enrollment key on the payment confirmation page, or in a confirmation email sent to the payer. If you're using Moodle to supplement a live classroom, you can put the Enrollment key on the syllabus. If you're using Moodle within a corporation, you can put the Enrollment key on your intranet where only employees can get it, or even have it physically delivered to their mailboxes.

Guest Access

Under the Site Settings page, you chose whether to allow guests into your site. If you chose to allow guests, the Front Page shows a Login as a guest button:

If you allow guests on your site, you can use the Guest access setting to allow guests into a course. This is useful for free courses, or when you want to allow people to look around a course before enrolling. Guests cannot post or submit content to a course. They can only read the course content.

Should You Allow Guest Access?

If the real value of a course is in the interaction, then you have little to lose by allowing guests to look around the course. If the real value is in the content that they read, then allowing guests might be giving too much away. Consider offering a free course instead.

Using Enrolment Key and Guest Access to Market Your Site

One of the best advertisements your site can have is a fully functioning sample course. However, if the only access to a sample course is Guest access, then potential students cannot post or submit content. They don't experience an interactive course. Instead of using Guest access for the sample course, consider this strategy:

Close your site to guest access. Explain on the Front Page, and on the Login Page (you'll learn how to customize that later) that users must create a free account to experience the fully functioning sample course. If you want to make this especially easy, don't require email confirmation when the student registers, but instead give instant approval. It requires no Enrollment key for your sample course. However, you do require an Enrollment key for paid courses. Now that the students in the sample course have user IDs, they can post to forums, take quizzes, enter journal entries, and upload content. Hopefully, experiencing this interaction will get them hooked on your courses. When they pay for a course, you supply them with an Enrollment key.

Cost

This field appears only if, under Administration | Enrolments, you select Paypal for the Primary method of enrollment. Selecting that option puts the Cost field in the Course Settings window.

In Administration | Enrolments, you selected an enrolment cost for the site, if any. On the Course Settings page, you can also enter a cost here for the specific course. If you enter any amount other than zero, when a student attempts to enroll in this course, the student is taken to a payment page at http://www.PayPal.com/. After the student pays, he or she is enrolled in the course and forwarded to the course's Home Page.

Hidden Sections

The setting Number of weeks/topics determines how many weeks or topics your course has. Each week or topic is a section. You can hide and reveal any section at will, except for Topic 0, which is always displayed. To hide and reveal a section, turn course editing on and click on the open or closed eye icon next to the section. The following example shows a course creator hiding and revealing section 1 of our sample course:

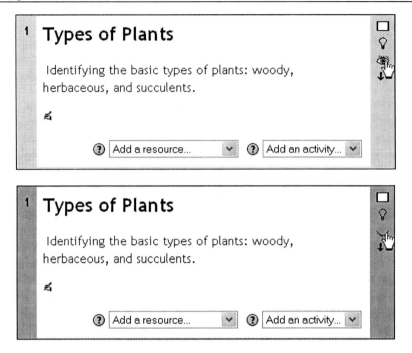

If you select Hidden sections are shown in collapsed form under Hidden Sections, then the titles or dates of sections that you have hidden will appear grayed out. The user cannot enter that section of the course, but does see that it is there. This is most useful if you plan to make sections of a course available in sequence, instead of making them available all at once. If you select Hidden sections are completely invisible, then hidden sections are invisible to students. Course creators and teachers can still see those sections and access the resources and activities in them.

News Items to Show

For Weekly and Topics course formats, a News forum automatically appears in a block on the right side of the course's Home Page:

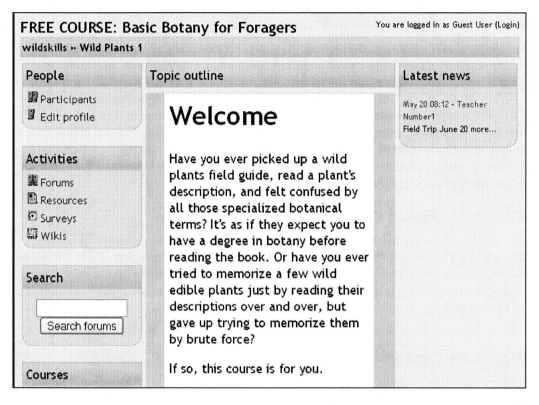

The News forum is like any other forum, except that it appears in the Latest news block. Like other forums, the course creator and editor can enable or disable the ability for students to create new topics, and to reply to existing topics.

The Latest news block automatically disappears if you have News items to show set to zero, or if there are no news items (no topics in the forum). Also, the Latest news block can be manually hidden, regardless of this setting or how many news items are posted.

> The maximum number of news item that the block will show is 10.

Show Grades and Show Activity Reports

These settings determine whether the grades and activities of each student can be seen by other students in the course. If your Group mode is set to Separate groups, then the reports are segregated by group. Regardless of this setting, teachers and administrators can always see the grade and activity reports.

For a course that allows guest access, setting this to Yes usually doesn't make much sense. Remember that every anonymous, unregistered user enters the course under the name *Guest*. So having a report that shows the grades and activities for Guest is usually not very useful. If you want to track how many people tried a sample course, and what parts of the course they sampled, allow users to create a free account to use in the fully functioning sample course. Make this especially easy by not requiring email confirmation when the student registers; instead give instant approval. Now, you can track and study individual usage in the sample course. To keep these anonymous users out of the courses requiring registration or payment, use a Login Page for those courses.

Maximum Upload Size

This setting limits the size of a file that a student can upload into this course. There is also a site-wide limit set under Administration | Configuration | Variables, in the maxbytes field. The smaller of the two settings: site-wide or course takes precedence here.

> The maximum you can select for this setting is 16MB

Words for Teacher and Student

Moodle inserts your term for teacher or student into its standard messages. For *Teacher*, you can substitute any term like *Instructor*, *Leader*, and *Facilitator*. For *Student*, you could use terms like *Participant* or *Member*.

Force Language

Selecting Do not force enables a student to select any language on the pull-down list of languages. Remember that the languages on the pull-down list are limited by the setting you chose for the langlist field under Administration | Configuration | Variables.

Also remember that only Moodle's standard menus and messages are automatically translated when a student selects a different language. Course material is not translated unless the course creator entered material in another language and used the Multi-language Content feature. If you want to show both Moodle menus/messages and course content in multiple languages, see the section dealing with the variable langlist.

Adding Teachers and Students

The easiest way to add teachers and students to a course is to use the Administration block:

Select Teachers (or Instructors, or whatever word your course uses for Teachers), or Students, and you will be taken to the Assign Teachers or Enrol Students screen. These screens list all authenticated users in the system. Any user can be made a teacher or student.

Before a user can be added as a teacher or student, the user must be authenticated.

Blocks can be turned on and off for each course, as covered in the following section called *Blocks*. If the Administration block is not displayed for this course, you will need to add students by going to the site's Front Page and selecting Administration | Users and then Enroll Students or Assign Teachers.

Blocks

A block displays information in a small area in one of the side columns. For example, a block can display a Calendar, the latest news, or the students enrolled in a course. Think of a block as a small applet. A block appears in the left or right column on the site's Front Page or a course's Home Page. A block does not appear when a course Resource or Activity is displayed.

When configuring the site, you can choose to display, hide, and position blocks on the site's Front Page. When configuring a course, you can also show/hide/position blocks on the course's Home Page. The procedure is the same whether working on the site's Front Page or a course's Home Page. We put this section on *Blocks* in the chapter on building courses, but it would have also been appropriate in the chapter on *Installing and Configuring Moodle*. We put it here because you will use this feature most often in the context of a course, and the site's Front Page is essentially a course. Before showing how to hide/show and position blocks, let's talk about what each block does and how you can use each block in your course.

The Standard Blocks

These blocks are available to you in a standard Moodle installation. You can also install additional blocks, available through http://moodle.org/.

Activities

The Activities block lists all of the types of activities available in the course:

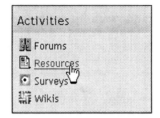

If the type of activity is not used in the course, the link for that type is not presented. When a user clicks on the type of activity, all the activities of that kind for the course are listed. If this block is on the site's Front Page, clicking on a type of activity gives a list for the activities on the Front Page (not for the entire site!). In the screenshot above, you can see that the course has at least one activity of each of the types Forums, Resources, Surveys, and Wikis. Other types of activities are not used in this course.

Administration

The most-used options that the Administration block presents a teacher, course creator, or administrator with are assigning teachers and enrolling students. In the following screenshot you can see the link Students. The screenshot was taken inside a course, by a user who is a teacher for that course. Therefore, the user can enroll students in this course. However, notice that the link for Instructors is not available to this teacher. On our sample learning site, only the site administrator can assign Instructors (teachers). Under Administration | Settings, the site administrator can choose to allow teachers to assign other teachers.

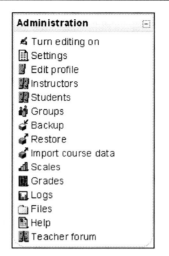

Backup and Restore do exactly what they are labeled: back up and restore the course.

Import course data enables the teacher to import the course material from any course that the teacher can access. The teacher can select from the different types of material: assignments, chats, forums, lessons, etc. It does not import the enrollment or record of activity from the course.

Scales enables a course creator or teacher to add evaluation scales to a course. When a scale is added to a course, it can then be used by students to rate forum postings, resources, activities, and assignments. This link appears in the Administration block only when viewing a course. When viewing the site's Front Page, this link is not available. A teacher can create a new scale or use a standard scale provided by the system administrator.

Grades displays grades for the students enrolled. Every activity and assignment that has grades enabled appears in the grading page. When viewing the site's Front Page, this link is not available. If you place a graded activity on the Front Page, like a quiz, and want to see the grades for that activity, you will need to select the activity itself and then select another link to view grades for that activity.

Logs displays the Administration | Logs page, where you select the information you want to extract from the site logs. Your choices are the same no matter what course you are in. You can display logs for the site, a selected course, a group, a student, a date, an activity, or any combination of these.

Files enables teachers and course creators to upload files to the course area. These files can then be linked to and used in the course. Course files can be seen by anyone enrolled in the course. When viewing the site's Front Page, this link is labeled Site files. Site files can be seen by any site user.

The Teacher forum is open only to those who have been assigned as teachers in this course.

Only teachers, course creators, and site administrators can see the Administration block. It is hidden from students. For that reason, there is very little disadvantage to having this block displayed. It appears on the Front Page and each course's Home Page by default. Consider keeping it unless you have a specific, compelling reason to hide it.

When this block appears on the site's Front Page, an Admin link appears at the bottom of the block. Clicking this takes the user to an Administration page with choices that apply to the entire site:

Administration

Configuration	Variables - Configure variables that affect general operation of the site
	Site settings - Define how the front page of the site looks
	Themes - Choose how the site looks (colors, fonts etc)
	Language - For checking and editing the current language pack
	Modules - Manage installed modules and their settings
	Blocks - Manage installed blocks and their settings
	Filters - Choose text filters and related settings
	Backup - Configure automated backups and their schedule
	Editor settings - Define basic settings for HTML editor
	Calendar - Configure various calendar and date/time-related aspects of Moodle
	Maintenance mode - For upgrades and other work
Users	Authentication - You can use internal user accounts or external databases
	Edit user accounts - Browse the list of user accounts and edit any of them
	Add a new user - To manually create a new user account
	Upload users - Import new user accounts from a text file
	Enrollments - Choose internal or external ways to control enrollments
	Enroll students - Go into a course and add students from the admin menu
	Assign teachers - Find a course then use the icon to add teachers 🔘
	Assign creators - Creators can create new courses and teach in them
	Assign admins - Admins can do anything and go anywhere in the site
Courses	Define courses and categories and assign people to them
Logs	Browse logs of all activity on this site
Site files	For publishing general files or uploading external backups

The options for site-wide administration are covered in other sections of this book. Look in the contents or index to locate more information about each of them.

Calendar

Workshops, assignments, quizzes, and events appear on the Calendar:

In the screenshot given, you can see that the user is pointing to an event that begins on the 20th. A pop-up window shows the name of the event (it is obscuring the first two rows of dates, which is common behavior for this block). This quiz was added to the Front Page, so it is a site-wide event.

When the course creator or administrator clicks on one of the four links at the bottom of the Calendar, it disables the display of that type of event. For example, if this Calendar is displayed on a course's Home Page, you might want to disable the display of global events and user events by clicking those links. This would result in the Calendar displaying only events for the course and the groups in the course.

Course Summary

The Course Summary block displays the course summary from the course's Settings page. This is the same course summary that is displayed when someone clicks the ❶ icon in the course listing, as shown overleaf. You can see the pop-up window that displays the course summary, and the course listing behind the popup. In this situation, the student has not yet entered the course, but instead is looking at the list of courses.

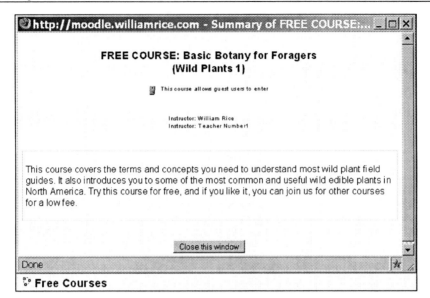

To enter a course, a student need only click the course name. A student might enter a course without clicking the ❶ icon. In that case, the student proceeds to the course's Home Page, without reading a course summary first. Displaying the Course Summary block on the course's Home Page gives the student another chance to see the course summary before proceeding with the course. In our sample course, it looks like this.

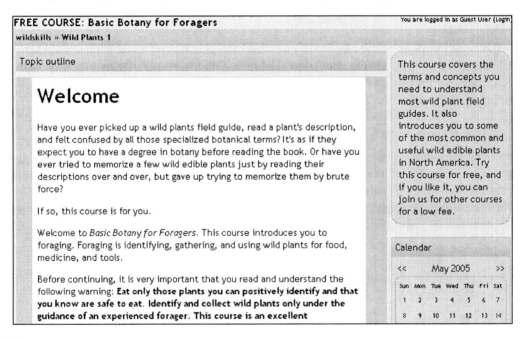

You could copy the course summary into Topic 0, so that it is the first item the students see. Then, the Course Summary block becomes redundant and you can use that space for something else, as I've done here:

FREE COURSE: Basic Botany for Foragers

You are logged in as Guest User (Login)

wildskills » Wild Plants 1

Topic outline

Latest news

Welcome

Course Summary

This course covers the terms and concepts you need to understand most wild plant field guides. It also introduces you to some of the most common and useful wild edible plants in North America. Try this course for free, and if you like it, you can join us for other courses for a low fee.

Course Description

Have you ever picked up a wild plants field guide, read a plant's description, and felt confused by all those specialized botanical terms? It's as if they expect you to have a degree in botany before reading the book. Or have you ever tried to memorize a few wild edible plants just by reading their descriptions over and over, but gave up trying to memorize them by brute force?

May 20 08:12 - Teacher Number1
Field Trip June 20 more...

Calendar

<<   May 2005   >>

Sun	Mon	Tue	Wed	Thu	Fri	Sat
1	2	3	4	5	6	7
8	9	10	11	12	13	14
15	16	17	18	19	20	21
22	23	24	25	26	27	28
29	30	31				

Global events   Course events

Courses

The Courses block displays links to the course categories. Clicking a link takes the student to the list of courses.

Courses

- Free Courses
- Wild Plants
- Tracking and Animal Observation
- Shelter and Fire

Search courses...
All courses...

This is useful if you want to enable students to move from course to course quickly, or want to encourage visitors to explore the site. However, you must balance this flexibility against using the space that the block occupies. Browser space is always precious. If you expect students to enter the course and stay there, then you may want to forego displaying this block. Instead, just display the list of courses on the Front Page.

Latest News

When you create a new course, by default it has a News forum. The Latest News block displays the most recent postings from this forum.

Even if the forum is renamed, this block displays the postings. The number of postings displayed in this block is determined in the Course Settings page, by the field News items to show. If this block is displayed on the site's Front Page, it displays the latest postings from the site-wide News forum.

If you have set the News forum to email students with new postings, you can be reasonably sure that the students are getting the news, so you might not need to display this block. However, if the news items are of interest to visitors not enrolled in the course, or if the course allows guest access, you probably want to display this block.

Login

The Login block is available only for the site's Front Page. After the user logs in, this block disappears. If a visitor is not logged in, Moodle displays small Login links in the upper-right corner and bottom center of the page. However, the links are not very noticeable. The Login block is much more prominent, and contains a message encouraging visitors to sign up for an account.

The main advantage to the Login block over the small Login links is the block's greater visibility. If you want to make the Login link in the upper-right corner larger, look in Moodle's index.php file for this line:

```
$loginstring = "<font size=2><a href=\"$wwwroot/login/index.php\">".get_
string("login")."</a></font>";
```

Change `<font size=2>` to a larger number. This increases the font size of the Login link.

If you want to edit the message displayed in the Login block, look for the string `startsignup` in the `moodle.php` file under the language folder. In my example site, I'm using the `language en_us`, so I look in the `file /lang/en_us/moodle.php` for this line:

```
$string['startsignup'] = 'Start now by creating a new account!';
```

Main Menu

The Main menu block is available only on the site's Front Page. Anything that can be added to a course can be added to this block, as you can see from the pull-down menus labeled Add a resource and Add an activity.

In my example site, I use the Main menu to convey information about the site and how to use the site. I want visitors to be able to easily get instructions for enrolling and using courses. Perhaps I should change the name of this block to How to Use this Site. I can do that by looking in the `moodle.php` file under the language folder for this line:

```
$string['mainmenu'] = 'Main menu';
```

Change `Main menu` to whatever you want displayed for the name of the menu.

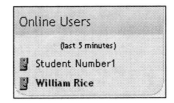

Online Users

The Online Users block shows who is on the site at the present time. Every few minutes, the block checks who is on the site.

You set the number of minutes under Administration | Configuration | Blocks | Online Users | Settings. Note that the users can be anywhere on the site; the block does not tell you where. For now, this does not offer a great advantage for students. Moodle does not have instant messaging. When it does, enabling your students to see who is online will be more useful.

People

When the People block is added to the site's Front Page, it lists the users enrolled on the site.

When it's added to a course, it lists the user enrolled in that specific course. If the site or course uses groups, it provides a link to those groups. It also provides a link to the user's profile page.

In the Site settings page, you use the showsiteparticipantslist field to determine who can see this list: students *and* teachers, or just teachers.

Recent Activity

When the Recent activity block is added to a course's Home Page, it lists all of the student and teacher activity in that course since the user's last login.

When added to the site's Front Page, it lists all of the student and teacher activity on the Front Page, but not in the individual courses, since the user's last login. If someone is logged in as a guest user, this block displays activity since the last time that Guest logged in. If guest users are constantly coming to your site, this block may be of limited use to them. One strategy is to omit this block from the site's Front Page, so anonymous users don't see it, and add it only to courses that require users to authenticate.

Remote RSS Feeds

When the Remote RSS Feeds block is added to a course, the course creator chooses or creates RSS feeds to display in that block.

The example above shows an RSS feed from an adventure racing site. This feed is the result of the configuration shown in the following screenshot:

```
wildskills » Administration » Configuration » Add/Edit Feeds
                    Feed                                Actions
4 Adventure Racing Info | 4AR.info                         ✎ ✗
http://feeds.feedburner.com/4AdventureRacingInfo4arinfo

        Update a news feed URL:
        http://feeds.feedburner.com/4AdventureRacingInfo4arinfo
        Custom title (leave blank to use title supplied by feed):
        4 Adventure Racing Info | 4AR.info
        [ Edit ]  Validate feed
```

A feed can be added by the site administrator, and then selected by the course creator for use in an RSS block. Or, when the course creator adds the RSS block, he or she can add a feed at that time. The new feed then becomes available to all other course creators, for use in all other courses. This is similar to the way quiz questions work. All quiz questions, no matter who created them, are available to all course creators for use in their courses.

Search

The Search block provides a search function for forums. It does not search other types of activities or resources. When this block is added to the site's Front Page, it searches only the forums on the Front Page.

```
Search

        [              ]
        [ Search forums ]
```

When it's added to a course's Home Page, it searches only the forums in that course. In Chapter 7, the section *Custom Strings* discusses how to customize Moodle's display strings, including the name of this box. You might want to change the name to Search forums to avoid giving the impression that it searches all content.

This block is different from the Search courses field that automatically appears on the site's Front Page. The Search courses field searches course names and descriptions, not forums.

Section Links

The Topics block displays links to the numbered topics or weeks in a course. Clicking a link advances the page to that topic. This block does not display the names of the topics. If you want to display links to the topics that show their names, you'll need to create those links yourself. The following screenshot shows an example of this:

Welcome

Course Summary

This course covers the terms and concepts you need to understand most wild plant field guides. It also introduces you to some of the most common and useful wild edible plants in North America. Try this course for free, and if you like it, you can join us for other courses for a low fee.

Course Description

Have you ever picked up a wild plants field guide, read a plant's description, and felt confused by all those specialized botanical terms? It's as if they expect you to have a degree in botany before reading the book. Or have you ever tried to memorize a few wild edible plants just by reading their descriptions over and over, but gave up trying to memorize them by brute force?

If so, this course is for you.

Welcome to *Basic Botany for Foragers*. This course introduces you to foraging. Foraging is identifying, gathering, and using wild plants for food, medicine, and tools.

Before continuing, it is very important that you read and understand the following warning: **Eat only those plants you can positively identify and that you know are safe to eat. Identify and collect wild plants only under the guidance of an experienced forager. This course is an excellent preparation for learning to identify plants under the guidance of an expert, but is not a substitute. You should learn under someone qualified and experienced in the collection of wild plants in your area. Common sense dictates that if you have any doubt as to a plant's safety, don't eat it.**

To learn more about this course, select *Course Goals and Outline* below. To meet your fellow foragers, join the *Course Discussion*. To jump into the course, just select a lesson.

Jump to a Topic

Types of Plants

Life Cycles of Plants

Leaves

Flowers

Roots

Other Identifying Features

Habitats

Here's one way to create those links:

While viewing the Home Page of the course, in the address bar of your browser you will see the web address of the course. In my example, it was `http://moodle.williamrice.com/course/view.php?id=4`. Select and copy this address.

1. In Topic 0, add a label. Do this by clicking the Add a resource drop-down menu and selecting Insert a label.

2. You should see a word processor-like window, where you enter the text of the label. In my example, I added a horizontal rule and then typed Jump to a Topic. You can add any text you want to introduce these links.

3. Type the name of the first topic, such as Types of Plants.

4. Select the name of the topic by dragging across it.

5. Click the ⊕ button to create the link. You should see a pop-up window where you enter the link.

6. In the Insert Link pop-up window, paste the link that you copied before. This is the link to the course's Home Page. Immediately after the link, type the hash sign (#) and the number of the topic or week. In the example below, I have highlighted the link to the course, which I copied earlier. I then type #1 to link to the first topic:

7. Repeat steps 4 through 6 for each topic.

8. When you're finished in the Edit label window, select the Save changes button to return to your course's Home Page. You will see the links in Topic 0.

Upcoming Events

The Upcoming Events block is an extension of the Calendar block. It gets event information from your calendar. By default, the Upcoming Events block displays 10 events; the maximum is 20. It looks ahead a default of 21 days; the maximum is 200. If there are more upcoming events than the maximum chosen for this block, the most distant events will not be shown.

Summary

Just as Moodle enables students to explore courses in a non-linear fashion, it also allows you to build courses in a flexible, nonlinear way. After you fill out the course settings page, the order in which you add material and features to your course is up to you. Don't get stuck if you don't know where to begin. For example, if you're unsure whether to use a Weekly or Topics format, just pick one and start adding material. If the course content begins to suggest a different type of course format, you can change the format later.

If your course is still under development when it's time to go live, use hidden sections to hide the unfinished portions. You can reveal them as you complete them.

When deciding which blocks to display, consider the comfort level of your students. If they're experienced web surfers, they may be comfortable with a full complement of blocks displaying information about the course. Experienced web surfers are adept at ignoring information they don't need (when was the last time you paid attention to a banner ad on the Web?). If your students are new computer users, they may assume that the presence of a block means that it requires their attention or interaction. And remember that you can turn blocks off and on as needed.

In general, make your best guesses when you first create a course, and don't let uncertainties about any of these settings stop you. Continue with the next chapter, *Adding Static Course Material*. As you add static, interactive, and social materials in the coming chapters, you can revisit the course structure and settings in this chapter and change them as needed.

4

Adding Static Course Material

Static course materials are resources that students read but don't interact with, such as web pages, graphics, and Adobe Acrobat documents. This chapter teaches you how to add those resources to a course, and how to make best use of them.

What Kinds of Static Course Material can be Added?

Static course material consists of resources that the student reads, but doesn't interact with. It is added from the Add a resource drop-down menu. Using this menu, you can create:

- Text pages
- Web pages
- Links to anything on the Web
- A view into one of the course's directories
- A label that displays any text or image

Links to these resources appear where you add the resource. The one exception is the label, which doesn't display a link. Instead, it displays the actual text or image that you put into the label.

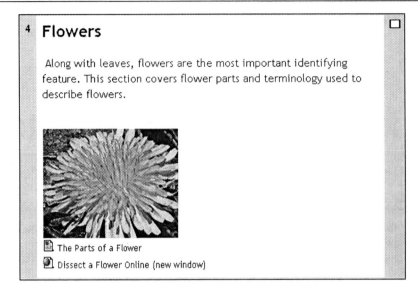

The example shown here is Topic 4 of our sample course, Flowers. The descriptive text immediately below Flowers is the topic summary, which was entered when the topic was created.

Below that, you can see a picture of a *Dandelion* flower. This picture was added as a label. The label can contain any text or picture that you want. However, you probably want to keep your labels small so that they don't dominate the course's Home Page. A single picture, a decorative divider, or a heading are the most common uses for a label.

Below the picture you can see a link to a web page created in Moodle, The Parts of a Flower. The page icon indicates this page is part of your Moodle site. Below that you can see a link to a web page that is outside of the Moodle site, Dissect a Flower Online. The world icon indicates this page is not part of your Moodle site. I indicate that link opens a new window by adding new window to its name.

The Resource Summary

When you create a new resource, you give it a name as shown. Unless it's a label, you also give it a summary. The other fields in the new resource window may change, but the name is always present and the summary is present for all except labels.

Link to a file or web site ⑦

Name:	Dissect a Flower Online (new window)

Summary:

Trebuchet ▾ | 3 (12 pt) ▾ | Normal ▾ | **B** *I* U S | x₂ x² | 📋 ✂ 📋 📝 | ↩ ↪

≡ ≡ ≡ ≡ | ⁋ ⁋ | ⁞≡ ⁞≡ ⁞≡ ⁞≡ | Tᵦ ◈ | — ♪ ⊕ ⊕ ▨ ▭ ☺ ◈ | ‹› | ◪

Summary ⑦

A virtual laboratory where you can dissect a flower, label it, and put it back together again. Produced by the British Broadcasting Corporation (BBC) and offered free on their school resources website.

Path: body » span.attribute-value

Location:	http://www.bbc.co.uk/schools/scienceclips/ages/9_10/life_cycles.shtml

Choose or upload a file ...	Search for web page ...

The name appears as the link to the resource. The summary appears only when the resource is shown in a list. To list the resources in a course, the student selects Resources from the Activities block.

Activities ❖ ✕ ← ↓

- 🗐 Forums
- 📄 Resources
- ◉ Surveys
- 🗇 Wikis

This means that the Activities block must be displayed for the course. If the course creator did not add the Activities block to the course, then the student cannot list the resources like this. When the student selects Resources, the Resources window appears, listing the resources in that course. In the next example, notice that the Topic number, Name, and Summary are shown for each resource:

	Topic	Name	Summary
		Course Goals and Outline	This is the outline and detailed course description for *Basic Botany for Foragers*.
	1	Types of Plants	## Types of Plants The first question that you will answer when identifying wild plants is, "What type of plant is it?" Botanists use a complex system called "taxonomy" to classify plants. The science of taxonomy enables botanists to classify and name the hundreds of thousands of plants on our planet. As foragers, we will use a simpler system. A common method of classifying plants is based on the habit, or appearance, of a plant. It is not as scientific or complete as taxonomy. However, this method is simple, easy to learn, and useful for quickly learning to identify wild plants. First, we classify plants as **woody**, **herbaceous**, or **succulent**. We define these terms here.
	4	The Parts of a Flower	This page shows you the parts of a flower. It divides the parts into two groups: those on the outside (leaves and petals) and those on the inside (reproductive parts).
		Dissect a Flower Online (new window)	A virtual laboratory where you can dissect a flower, label it, and put it back together again. Produced by the British Broadcasting Corporation (BBC) and offered free on their school resources website.

wildskills » Wild Plants 1 » Resources

Activities Block Encourages Exploration

As you can see from the screenshot of the Activities block, it contains links that display all activity types in the course.

Among these activities are the static resources covered in this chapter. When the student selects Resources, he or she sees a list of all the text pages, web pages, links, and files in this course. This can make it easier for students to find resources in a long course.

The items listed by the Activities block do not appear in context. If you are requiring students to proceed through a course in sequence, you may want to hide this block. If you want to encourage exploration in the course, it is a good block to display.

Files

Moodle enables anyone with course-creator privileges to upload files to the site, or to an individual course. This is done with the Site files link in the Administration block. The Site files link appears only for users with course creator privileges, so the ability to add site-wide or course-wide files is hidden from students and teachers.

Note that uploading a file is different from uploading an assignment. When a course creator uploads a file, it is with the intention that the file will be used in the course. When a student uploads an assignment, it is with the intention that it will be graded by the teacher.

Why Upload Files?

When a file is added from a course's Home Page, links to the file can easily be created within that course. When a file is added from the site's Front Page, a course creator can easily create links to that file from anywhere on the Front Page. (Remember that the site's Front Page is really just another course.) This ease of creating links is one of the advantages to uploading files to Moodle, instead of linking to them on the Web.

Another advantage to using uploaded files is that Moodle enables you to easily rename and move the files. Notice the Rename links in the screenshot overleaf. Also, I can select any of these files, and from the With chosen files drop-down list, move them to any other course in Moodle.

In the example, I've added files to the course called FreePics. The navigation links across the top of the page indicate that I started at the site's Front Page (wildskills), selected the course FreePics, and then from the Administration block selected Files. I then uploaded the seven image files.

File Types

You can upload any kind of file into Moodle. Remember that the file will be accessed by the user's web browser, so consider whether the user's web browser can open the file. Images, MP3 files, Flash files, Adobe Acrobat documents, and other file types commonly found on the Web are a safe bet for uploaded files.

You may want to upload a file that cannot be opened by a web browser. In that case, the file must be opened by an application on the user's computer. For example, if you're teaching a course on architecture, you might add AutoCAD drawings to your course. The students' browsers probably cannot open AutoCAD files. Instead, the students would need to download the drawings to their computers, and then open them with AutoCAD. If you do something like this, indicate in the link that the students should download the file to their computers. For example, you might instruct them to right-click and select Download or Save file.

Linking to Uploaded Files

Linking to an uploaded file is easy. From anywhere in the course, select the Add a resource drop-down menu and select Link to a file or web site:

Free Wilderness Pictures

This course is a holding place for free wilderness pictures. Guests and students are free to use these pictures in their wilderness studies, for screen savers and backgrounds, in electronic art, school reports...however you like. Browse and enjoy!

Regards,

William Rice

✍

🎓 News forum ➡ ⬆ ✍ ✕ ☀ 🔒

(?) | Add a resource... ▾ | (?) | Add an activity... ▾ |

---

1 Wild Plants

✍

(?) | Add a resource... ▾ | (?) | Add an activity... ▾ |

| Add a resource... |
| Compose a text page |
| Compose a web page |
| **Link to a file or web site** |
| Display a directory |
| Insert a label |

---

2 Wild Animals

✍

The Editing Resource window appears:

Link to a file or web site ⑦

Name: Common Burdock in the Spring

Summary: | Trebuchet ▾ | 3 (12 pt) ▾ | Normal ▾ | **B** *I* U S | x₂ x² | ... |

Summary ⑦

Burdock is one of the first wild plants available in the spring. Its roots left over from the winter are a good source of nutrition.

Path: body

Location: burdock_sprout_spring.png

| Choose or upload a file ... | | Search for web page ... |

1. Enter a Name for the link. This is the text that will be displayed for the user.
2. The Summary will be displayed when this link appears in a list of resources.
3. If you were linking to a file on the Web, you would enter the URL (web address) into the Location field. To link to an uploaded file, select the Choose or upload a file button.
4. The Files window appears. Next to the file you want to link to, select Choose:

FreePics » Files			
Name	**Size**	**Modified**	**Action**
☐ 🖾 burdock_sprout_spring.png	1.1Mb	27 May 2005, 07:54 AM	Choose Rename

5. Click the Save changes button.
6. The file is displayed in its own window, as the students will see it. You are now seeing what students will see when they click on the link to the file.

To return to the course, select the course name from the navigation bar. Back at the course, you will see the link you created.

Why Use Uploaded Files?

Upload files into Moodle when:

- You want a file to be used several places in the course. Creating links to an uploaded file is easy, and if you change the file it will be updated in all places in the course.

- You need to ensure that you have control over the file. Linking to a file on another web page outside of Moodle puts the author of that web page in control of the content. Bringing the file into Moodle ensures that only the people you want can change the file.

- You might want to use the file in another course. Moodle's file window enables you to copy and move files between courses.

Text Page

Under the Add a resource drop-down menu, use Compose a text page to add a text page to any course, including the site's Front Page. A link then appears to the page that you have created. The page is stored in Moodle's database.

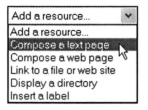

The name "text page" implies an unformatted, text-only page. However, Moodle's text pages can take several formats. Each of these formats offers some advantages and disadvantages.

The online help explains what each format is, and how to use it. This section covers when to use each of the text page formats:

- Moodle auto-format
- Plain text format
- Markdown format

Formatting

There are three types of formats you can use while creating a new text page. Each offers some advantages and disadvantages. They all offer a limited set of formatting commands. If you need more formatting options, add a web page instead of a text page.

Moodle Auto-Format: for Quick, Limited Formatting

The Moodle auto-format offers a simple way to add limited formatting to a text page. It automatically turns codes into *smilies*, such as turning :-) into a smiley. It turns any word starting with www or http:// into a clickable link. It also enables you to add some HTML tags for text formatting, such as bold, underline, and font size.

You can see that its only real advantage over plain text is a few formatting commands. However, you will need to learn the HTML tags for these formats. If you're going to learn these HTML commands, you may as well add an HTML (web) page instead. Then later, when you learn more than these simple HTML commands, you can return to the web page and add to it.

Plain Text Format: for Program Listings

This is true, unformatted, plain text. It displays your text exactly as you type it. A plain text page is especially useful for presenting a large block of computer code exactly as you write it.

Markdown Format: Intuitive, Fast Formatting

If you don't already know Wiki formatting commands, and you just want to quickly create formatted text pages, Markdown format offers a good alternative. Its set of commands is larger than the Moodle auto-format but smaller than Wiki or HTML. It's also intuitive. Writing in Markdown format is meant to be fast and simple. For example, the following is a fourth-level heading followed by a list in Markdown format:

```
####Trees
* A single trunk, which might fork above ground.
* Trunk is 3 or more inches in diameter.
* Over 16 feet tall, under favorable growing conditions.
```

It gets displayed like the list below:

Trees

- A single trunk, which might fork above ground.
- Trunk is 3 or more inches in diameter.
- Over 16 feet tall, under favorable growing conditions.

Window Settings

The bottom of the text editing page displays window settings. By default, the text page is displayed in the top frame of the Moodle window. You can use the window settings to make the page display in its own window, and to control the look and size of that window.

When to Open Pages in a New Window?

If you make the page open in its own window, and this is not the usual behavior for resources on your site, the student who opens this page might not realize that he or she has opened a new window. Adding new window to the end of the page's name can avoid this confusion. For example, I might name my page like this:

If your pages usually open in a new window, or if you resize the new window so that it does not obscure the original Moodle site beneath it, this isn't necessary. Just make sure that the behavior the users sees when opening a new text page is consistent across your site.

Web Page

You can compose web pages in Moodle, and also copy and paste HTML code from other web pages into Moodle. Web pages give you more options than any of the text document types covered above, including the ability to include Java and other active code on the page. To start creating a web page, from the Add a resource drop-down menu, choose the option Compose a web page.

You do not need to learn HTML to create web pages in Moodle. When you compose a web page, Moodle gives you a WYSIWYG (What You See Is What You Get) word processor on screen. This word processor gives you basic formatting icons in the toolbar. Pointing to any icon displays a popup telling you the name of the command:

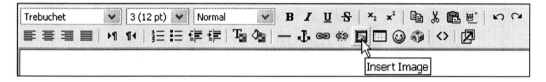

You can see from the icons on the toolbar that Moodle's built-in editor enables you to:

- Select the font face and size
- Tag paragraphs as Normal, Heading, Preformatted, and Address
- Create superscripts and subscripts
- Align paragraphs
- Increase/decrease paragraph spacing
- Create bulleted and numbered lists
- Indent and outdent paragraphs
- Insert horizontal lines
- Create anchors on the page
- Link to other web resources and anchors on this page
- Insert images
- Create tables
- Insert smilies
- Insert special characters

Advantages of Using HTML View When Editing Web Pages

This is quite a list of formatting commands. However, there are many more things that you can do in HTML that cannot be done through these icons. To do more, you must view and edit the raw HTML code. To access the HTML code, click the View HTML button <>. The following two screenshots show the same page in WYSIWYG and HTML view:

Tree, Shrub, What's the Difference?

Many people can't say exactly what the difference is between a tree and a shrub, but, they know it when they see it! Since many field guides use the terms "tree" and "shrub" we'll define them here.

Trees vs. Shrubs

Shrub	Tree
Multiple trunks that fork underground or at ground level.	A single trunk, which might fork above ground.
Trunk or stem is less than 3 inches in diameter.	Trunk is 3 or more inches in diameter.
Less than 16 feet tall, under favorable growing conditions.	Over 16 feet tall, under favorable growing conditions.
Others may differ on these definitions.	

Examples

Path: body » table » tbody » tr » td » ul » li

```
<h3>Tree, Shrub, What's the Difference?</h3>

<p>Many people can't say exactly what the difference is between a tree
and a shrub, but, they know it when they see it! Since many field
guides use the terms &quot;tree&quot; and &quot;shrub&quot; we'll
define them here.</p>

<table summary="This table lists the characteristics of shrubs and
trees, and how they differ.">

<caption>Trees vs. Shrubs</caption>
<thead>
<tr>
<th id="header1">Shrub</th>
<th id="header2">Tree</th>
</tr>
</thead>

<tfoot>
<tr>
<td class="centered" colspan="2">Others may differ on these
definitions. </td>
</tr>
</tfoot>

<tbody>
```

Notice that in the HTML code I've included features in the table that are not available in Moodle's (or most programs) WYSIWYG HTML editor. The table has a summary, caption, column IDs assigned to the headers, and footer. To add these more advanced HTML features, I had to go into HTML view.

Composing in an HTML Editor and Uploading to Moodle

For long or complex HTML pages, or just for your own comfort, you might want to compose your web page in an HTML editor like **DreamWeaver** or **FrontPage**. This is especially true if you want to take advantage of these editors' ability to insert JavaScript timing, and other advanced features into your web page. How then do you get that page into your Moodle course? You can copy and paste the HTML code from your web page editor into the Moodle page editing window. To do this you would:

- Select HTML view in your web page editor. For example, in DreamWeaver you would select View | Code, and in FrontPage you would select View | Reveal Codes.

- Select the HTML code in your web page, between the two body tags. That is, drag from just after the <body> tag near the top, to just before the </body> tag at the end.

- Copy the code with Edit | Copy or pressing *Ctrl+C*.
- Switch over to Moodle, and create the new web page.
- Show the HTML code by clicking the <> icon.
- Paste the code by pressing *Ctrl+V*.

A second method is to publish your web page to someplace outside of Moodle, and create a link to it from your course.

Learn More about HTML

To learn more about HTML code, you can start with the organization responsible for defining the standards. The World Wide Web Consortium maintains the complete standards for HTML online at `http://www.w3.org/TR/html4`. It maintains a basic tutorial at `http://www.w3.org/MarkUp/Guide/`. Everything covered in this basic guide can be done using the WYSIWYG tools in Moodle. The advanced HTML guide at `http://www.w3.org/MarkUp/Guide/Advanced.html` covers some features that you would need to go into HTML view to add. For example:

- Flowing text around images
- Defining clickable regions within images
- Using roll-overs

Link

On your Moodle site, you can show other content from anywhere on the Web by using a link. You can also link to files that you've uploaded into your course. By default, this content appears in a frame within your course. You can also choose to display it in a new window.

When using content from outside sites, you need to consider the legality and reliability of using the link. Is it legal to display the material within a window on your Moodle site? Will the material still be there when your course is running? In this example, I've linked to an online resource from the BBC, which is a fairly reliable source:

Remember that the bottom of the window displays Window Settings, so you can choose to display this resource in its own window. You can also set the size of the window. You may want to make it appear in a smaller window, so that it does not completely obscure the window with your Moodle site. This will make it clearer to the student that he or she has opened a new window.

When to Use a Link versus a Web Page

In the previous screenshot, you see the link Summary entered by the course creator. The student will not see this summary when clicking on the link. Instead, the student is taken directly to the location of the link. The student will only see the summary after selecting Resources from the Activities block. Then, all of the web pages, text pages, and links in the course will be listed with their summaries. The link will be listed like this:

Dissect a Flower Online (new window)	A virtual laboratory where you can dissect a flower, label it, and put it back together again. Produced by the British Broadcasting Corporation (BBC) and offered free on their school resources website.

If you want the student to always see a description of the link before proceeding to the resource, create a web page and put the link on the page. For example, I added a web page using the Add a resource drop-down menu and selecting Compose a web page. I filled out the edit web page window like this:

Compose a web page ⑦

Name: Dissect a Flower Online

Summary:
Summary ⑦

Trebuchet | 1 (8 pt) | | B *I* U S | x₂ x² | ✂ 📋 | ↶ ↷
≡ ≡ ≡ ≡ | ¶ ¶ | ≔ ≔ ⯈ ⯇ | — ⚓ 🔗 | 🖼 ☺ | ◇ | 🗗

Link to a virtual laboratory where you can dissect a flower, label it, and put it back together again.

Path:

Full text:
Write carefully ⑦
How to write text ⑦
Use emoticons ☺

Trebuchet | 1 (8 pt) | | B *I* U S | x₂ x² | ✂ 📋 | ↶ ↷
≡ ≡ ≡ ≡ | ¶ ¶ | ≔ ≔ ⯈ ⯇ | — ⚓ 🔗 | 🖼 ☺ | ◇ | 🗗

A virtual laboratory where you can dissect a flower, label it, and put it back together again. Produced by the British Broadcasting Corporation (BBC) and offered free on their school resources website. Click here to open the page in a new window.

The result on the course's Home Page is a link to this web page:

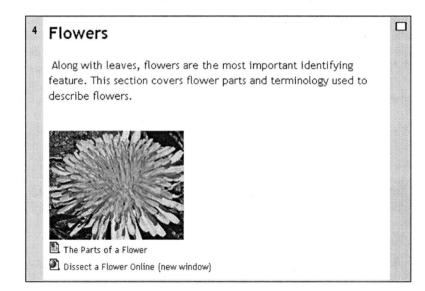

The resulting web page looks like this:

```
FREE COURSE: Basic Botany for Foragers
                  ‹  | Jump to...                          ▼ | ›
wildskills » Wild Plants 1 » Resources » Dissect a Flower Online

   A virtual laboratory where you can dissect a flower, label it, and put it back together
   again. Produced by the British Broadcasting Corporation (BBC) and offered free on their
   school resources website. Click here to open the page in a new window.



                   Last modified: Wednesday, August 10 2005, 11:32 AM




                   You are logged in as Student Number1 (Logout)
                          |    Wild Plants 1    |
```

Directory

Adding a directory to a course is another way to display the files that you have uploaded
to a course. Under the subsection Files, you saw that in the same window where you
upload files to a course you can create folders:

Free Wild Pictures

Logou

wildskills » FreePics » Files

Name	Size	Modified	Action
☐ 🖻 burdock_sprout_spring.png	1.1Mb	27 May 2005, 07:54 AM	Rename
☐ 🖻 burdock_summmer.png	1.4Mb	27 May 2005, 07:54 AM	Rename
☐ 🖻 dandelion_leaves_spring.png	1.9Mb	27 May 2005, 07:55 AM	Rename
☐ 🖻 field_garlic_sprouts_spring.png	820.1Kb	27 May 2005, 07:55 AM	Rename
☐ 🖻 nettle_summmer.png	1.1Mb	27 May 2005, 07:58 AM	Rename
☐ 🖻 thistle_summer_photo.png	1.2Mb	27 May 2005, 07:58 AM	Rename
☐ 🖻 yarrow_summmer.png	1.7Mb	27 May 2005, 07:58 AM	Rename

| With chosen files... ▼ | | Make a folder | Upload a file |

When you add a directory to a course, you're adding a link to the main files area or to one of the folders that you created. The directory resource creates a link on the course's Home Page, with a folder icon, like this:

When a student clicks the directory, the contents are displayed:

Why Use a Directory?

The other way to give students access to uploaded files is by creating a link to each individual file. For creating a link to several files, adding a directory is easier and simpler. If students need to download several files for a course, you can upload the files, put those files into a folder, and then create a directory to give them access to all the files. Also, a directory provides a level of organization for the files you supply to the student.

Label

Topic and weekly courses are organized into sections. Labels can help you organize material within a section, giving you another level of organization. A label can have any amount text, image, or other content that you can put on a web page. It is essentially an HTML document. However, just because a label can handle any HTML content, you don't want to go overboard and create entire web pages in a label. A label's main purpose is to add organization to a course's Home Page.

In the next screenshot you can see that the Wild Plants course uses labels to organize course resources. The horizontal lines and Jump to a topic, Group Activities, and Before You Start the Course: Do These Activities headlines are labels:

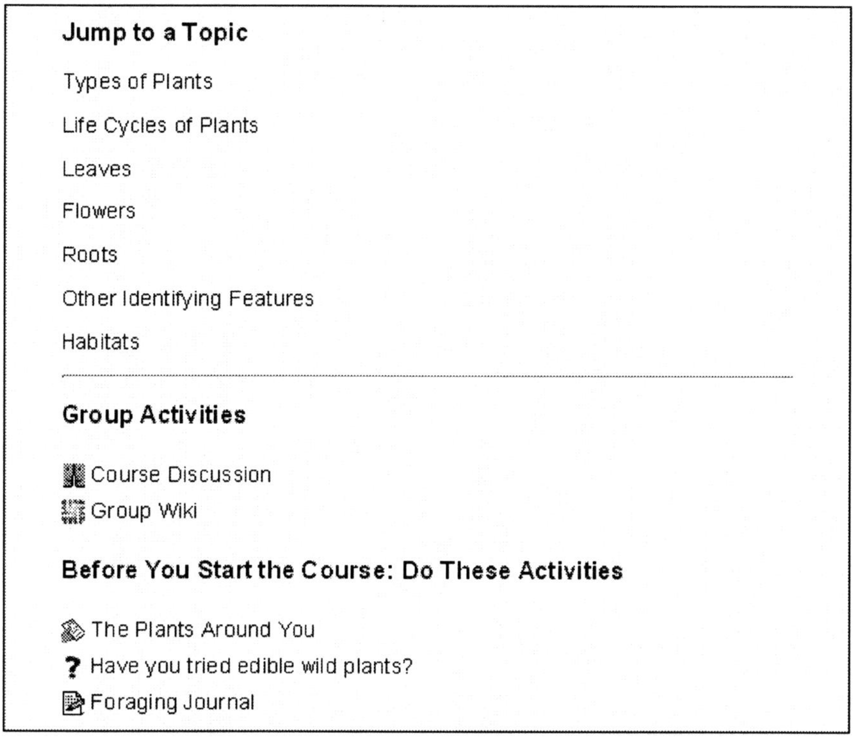

Jump to a Topic

Types of Plants

Life Cycles of Plants

Leaves

Flowers

Roots

Other Identifying Features

Habitats

Group Activities

▊ Course Discussion

▧ Group Wiki

Before You Start the Course: Do These Activities

▨ The Plants Around You

? Have you tried edible wild plants?

▤ Foraging Journal

In our example, the course creators used text labels to organize the course content. A label can also hold a graphic. Adding a graphic to the beginning of each topic is a good way to add visual interest to a course. Also, a label can consist of a large amount of text. You can introduce activities with a paragraph-long label. In the screenshot shown, perhaps a sentence explaining each activity would help the student understand the course flow. That can be added with a label. Make creative use of labels for organization, interest, and information.

Summary

These five static course materials (text pages, web pages, links, directory views, and labels) form the core of most online courses. Most student/teacher interaction will be about something the student has read or viewed. Adding static material first gives you a chance to think about how the material will be discussed and used. In later chapters, you'll see how to add more interactive material.

5

Adding Interactive Course Material

Interactive course activities enable students to interact with the instructor, the learning system, or each other. Note that Moodle doesn't categorize activities into "Interactive" and "Static" as we do in this book. In Moodle, all activities are added from the Add an activity menu, after Turn editing on. We use the terms "Interactive" and "Static" as a convenient way to categorize the activities that Moodle offers.

The table below gives you a brief description of each kind of activity. The sections after that describe how and when to use these activities.

Activity	Description
Assignment	An assignment is an activity completed offline, outside of Moodle. When the student completes the assignment, (s)he either uploads a file for the instructor's review or reports to the instructor in some other way. Regardless of whether the assignment requires uploading a file, the student receives a grade for the assignment.
Choice	A choice is essentially a single, multiple-choice question that the instructor asks the class. The result can be displayed to the class, or kept between the individual student and instructor. Choices are a good way to get feedback from the students about the class. You can plant these choices in your course ahead of time, and keep them hidden until you need the students' feedback. You can also add them as needed.
Journal	You can create an online journal for each student. A journal can be seen only by the student who writes it, and the instructor. Remember that a journal is attached to the course in which it appears. If you want to move a student's journal to another course, you'll need to make creative usage of the backup and restore functions.

Activity	Description
Lesson	A lesson is a series of web pages displayed in a given order, where the next page displayed depends upon the student's answer to a question. Usually, the "jump question" is used to test a student's understanding of the material. Get it right, and you proceed to the next item. Get it wrong, and you either stay on the page or jump to a remedial page. But the jump question could just as easily ask a student what (s)he is interested in learning next, or some other exploratory question.
	A lesson gives Moodle some of the branching capability found in commercial computer-based training (CBT) products. You could make a course consisting of just a summary, one large lesson, and a quiz.
Quiz	Quizzes and questions that you add to one course can be reused in other courses. We'll cover creating question categories, creating questions, and choosing meaningful question names.
SCORM	SCORM (Sharable Content Object Reference Model) is a collection of specifications that enable interoperability, accessibility, and reusability of web-based learning content. If a piece of learning material meets the SCORM standard, it can be inserted into any learning management system that supports SCORM (which is most of the major ones). Moodle's SCORM module allows you to upload any standard SCORM package into your course.
Survey	Moodle comes with prewritten surveys, designed by educational experts to help instructors learn about their students. If the stock survey questions are not appropriate for your usage, you have two choices: repurpose a quiz into a survey, or edit the survey's PHP code to change the questions. This section covers using the stock surveys, and those two options for custom surveys.

Wikis and Workshops are covered in the next chapter.

Assignments

After logging in as a teacher, and turning on editing, you can add an assignment from the Add an activity menu. This brings up the Editing Assignment window:

Assignment name: The Plants Around You

Description:

Write carefully ⑦
Ask good questions ⑦
About the HTML editor ⑦

| Trebuchet | 1 (8 pt) | | **B** *I* U S | x₂ x² | 🖹 ✂ 📋 📋 | ↶ ↷ |

that park you pass every day? What kind of flowering plant is growing in that field across from where you work?

Upload a picture of a plant or a green area that interests you. **The picture must have sufficient detail to identify the plant(s) in it.**

If you have a digital camera, this is easy. If not, you can take any copyright-free plant picture you find on the Web (government sites are good for this) and upload it.

The instructor for this course will put the pictures into an album, and try to identify the plant(s) for you.

Path: body

Grade: 10 ⑦

Available from: ☐ 7 May 2006 - 22 35

Due date: ☑ 2 November 2006 - 22 50

Prevent late submissions: No

Assignment type: Upload a single file ⑦

Next » Cancel

The Assignment name field is displayed on the course page. When a student clicks on the name, the Description field is displayed. The description should give complete directions for completing and submitting the assignment.

Assignments that are due soon will appear in the Upcoming Events block (covered in Chapter 3). If you do not set a due date, by default it will be set to today (the day you created the assignment). This will make the assignment show up the Upcoming Events block, as if it's overdue. Make sure you set an appropriate due date for the assignment.

Printer-Friendly Directions

Because assignments are completed offline, you may want the directions to be printer-friendly so that students can take the directions with them. Make sure that any graphics you've embedded into the Description field are less than the width of the printed page. Or, you can upload the directions as an **Adobe Acrobat** (.pdf) file, and use the Description field to instruct students to print the directions and take the directions with them.

Make it Clear Assignments are Mandatory

On the course's Home Page, an assignment link appears with its own icon, like this: 📚. It is not immediately apparent to a new student that this icon means "Do this assignment." You might want to use a label to indicate that the assignment is something the student should do. In this example, a label instructs the student to complete the assignment and a multiple-choice survey question:

Before You Start the Course: Do These Activities
📚 The Plants Around You
? Have you tried edible wild plants?

Assignments also appear in the Upcoming Events block. Even if you have no other events planned for the course (like a field trip, discussion, chat, etc.), if you have an assignment consider adding the Upcoming Events block. This will serve as an additional reminder for the students. Also, if you display the Recent Activity block, content that was recently added or edited will appear in that block. If you add or edit an assignment while the course is underway, the Recent Activities block will serve as an additional reminder to complete the assignment.

Choices

A Choice activity is designed to be a single, multiple-choice survey question that you pose to the class. Students choose one of the choices that you present. This is meant to be faster and more spontaneous than a survey. You can use a Choice activity to stimulate thinking about a topic, to find out how the students feel about the direction of the course, or to get the class's agreement on next steps.

In the editing screen shown in the following figure, notice that you can restrict the activity to a given time period:

Choice name: Have you tried edible wild plants?

Choice text:

Trebuchet | 1 (8 pt) | Normal | **B** *I* U S

Write carefully ⑨
Ask good questions ⑨
About the HTML editor ⑨

Here's a survey question for our new students: Have you tried eating any edible wild plants?

Path: body » p

Choice 1: Yes, I've tried edible plants found in the wild. ⑨ **Limit:** 0

Choice 2: No, not yet. ⑨ **Limit:** 0

Choice 3: Sort of. They were plants that you can find in the wild, but I bought ⑨ **Limit:** 0

Choice 4: ⑨ **Limit:** 0

Choice 5: ⑨ **Limit:** 0

Limit the number of responses allowed: ⑨ Disable

Restrict answering to this time period: ☐ ⑨

Open: 7 | May | 2006 | 22 | 40
Until: 7 | May | 2006 | 22 | 40

Display Mode: Display horizontally

Publish results: Always show results to students

Privacy of results: Publish anonymous results, do not show student names

Allow choice to be updated: Yes

Show column for unanswered: No

Group mode: No groups ⑨

Visible to students: Show

Save changes | Cancel

You are logged in as William Rice (Logout)

Wild Plants 1

Under Publish results, you can choose whether to show the results of the survey, and when. Remember that this is affected by the Group setting. If you choose separate groups for the course or for this activity, then each group will see only its own results.

Under Privacy of results, you select whether to include the students' names with their responses. The list can get long, so consider carefully before enabling this for a large class.

Allow choice to be updated enables a student to go back and change his or her response to the question.

Show column for unanswered determines whether the results will include students who are enrolled in the course and group, but did not answer the question. This can be useful when a question is used to vote on how the course is proceeding. Students may want to know if the majority of students in class have voted.

Journal

A Journal is private, between the student and the instructor. If you want to add a group Journal to a course, add a Wiki. A Wiki is by nature collaborative, and makes a good tool for group work.

Each Journal is a single online page, of almost unlimited length. When the Moodle documentation talks about "journal topics", the implication is that you will create a separate Journal for each topic. However, if you want students to write about several topics in a single Journal, you can instruct them to use headings to separate the topics.

You can assign a Journal a number of points to be graded, or make it ungraded. You can also choose to have the Journal open for a number of weeks after you create it.

Lesson

A Lesson is the most complex, and most powerful, type of activity. Essentially, a Lesson is a series of web pages that presents information and questions. Usually, each page in a lesson is short, and ends with one or a few questions about the material on that page. Depending upon the student's answer, the student is taken to another page. A correct answer advances the student to the next page, further into the topic. An incorrect answer either repeats the current page, or sends the student to a remedial page.

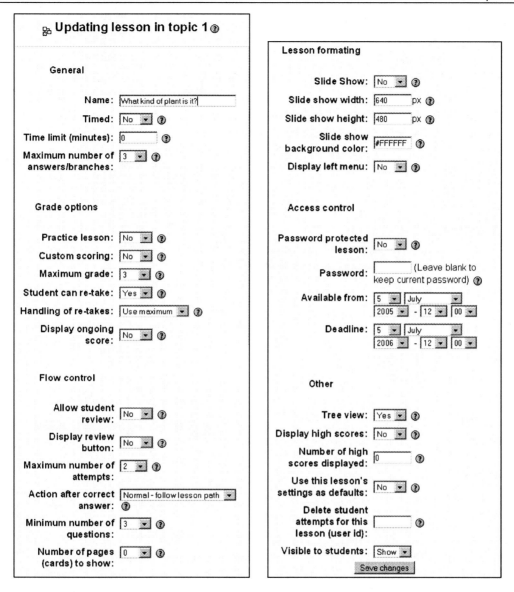

When you are creating a Lesson, you see all of the pages in the Lesson in their logical order. The logical order is the order in which a student would see them, if the student answered every question correctly and proceeded straight through the lesson. At any time, you can preview the lesson from the student's point of view. This section will cover previewing a lesson.

A lesson can be graded or ungraded. It also can allow students to retake the Lesson. While Moodle allows you to grade a Lesson, remember that a lesson's primary purpose is to teach, not test. Don't use a Lesson to do the work of a Quiz or Assignment. The lesson's score is there to give you a feedback on the effectiveness of each page, and to enable the students to judge their progress.

The Lesson Settings

When you first create a lesson, you are presented with a window where you choose settings for the entire lesson. This window is broken into six areas:

- General
- Grade options
- Flow control
- Lesson formatting
- Access control
- Other

We will cover each area in a subsection below. The focus will be on how the choices you make in each area affect the student and teacher experience.

General

The Name is displayed on the course Home Page. When a student clicks the name, the student is taken to the first page in the lesson.

Timed determines if the student has set a time limit to complete the lesson. If you select Yes, you must then set the time limit. When the student begins the lesson, a timer is displayed. If the time runs out before the student finishes the lesson, the student can keep going. However, any questions answered after the time runs out do not count towards the student's score.

The Maximum number of answers/branches sets the maximum number of answers available for each question. You don't need to use all the answers for every question. For example, if you set this to 3, then any question in this lesson can have one, two, or three choices. You can change this value while working on the lesson.

Grade Options

If Practice lesson is set to Yes, the score for this lesson does not show up in the site's grade book.

Normally, each correct answer in the lesson is worth the same number of points: the Maximum grade divided by the number of correct answers. Each incorrect answer is worth zero points. When you select Yes for Custom scoring, you decide what each answer is worth. You can assign points to correct and incorrect answers, and they can be negative or positive points.

The Maximum grade is for the entire lesson. Usually, you make the Maximum grade divisible by the number of correct answers in the lesson. For example, if all the questions from all the pages in the lesson have a total of four correct answers, you might assign a maximum grade of 4, 8, or 12 points.

User can re-take determines if a student can take the lesson more than once. Because lessons are meant for teaching instead of testing, the default value is Yes. If you're using a lesson as a test, you can set this to No. In the next parameter, Handling of re-takes, you decide if the student's grade is the average of all takes, or the best from all takes.

Display ongoing score turns on or off the display of a message that tells the student how many points (s)he has attempted and earned. For example, it might display, "This is a 20 point lesson, you have earned 5 of 10 points attempted so far."

Flow Control

Flow control options affect the student's ability to review and move through the lesson.

Allow student review determines if the student can navigate back through the lesson and review his/her answers. Leaving this set to Yes may encourage students to explore the different answers and branches in a lesson.

Display review button displays a button after a student submits an incorrect answer. The student can click the button and try the question again. If you're using the lesson as an exam, this should be set to No. But if you'd like to encourage the student to explore and learn, consider setting this to Yes.

Maximum number of attempts determines the maximum number of times a student can attempt to answer any question in the lesson. It affects all questions in the lesson. If a question doesn't have an answer to display, such as a short answer or essay question, Moodle displays a link to the next page instead. If you set this to 1 attempt, your lesson becomes a quiz with each question displayed on its own page.

Action after correct answer is the difference between a normal lesson, where the student proceeds through the pages in order, and a flash card lesson. Normally, when a student selects a correct answer, the lesson displays the next page of the lesson. The default for this setting, Normal – follow lesson path, enables this. The other two options for this setting turn the lesson into a flash card session.

Show an unseen page displays any page that the user has not seen. The order in which these are displayed is random. For example, if you are teaching a vocabulary, and each word has only one card, this option would display each vocabulary word only once. Displaying each page only once might not be the best choice for teaching new material, but it does enable the lesson to act as a random question quiz.

Selecting Show an unanswered page makes the lesson display only pages the student has not correctly answered. If the student answered a question incorrectly, it might be shown again.

Number of pages (cards) to show is used only when you've chosen to make your lesson behave as flash cards. Setting this to either zero or a number greater than the number of cards in the lesson shows all the cards in the lesson. Any number between zero and the number of cards in the lesson results in exactly that number of cards being shown to the student.

Lesson Formatting

The settings in this area affect the size and style with which the lesson is displayed.

Slide show enables the display of the lesson as a slide show. Each page becomes a slide. The lesson will appear in a new window. The width and height settings determine the size of the slide show window. If the window is too small to display the slide, the window displays a scroll bar. Only pages are displayed in the slide window. Questions are still shown in the main Moodle window.

The background color setting uses the Web's 6-letter code for colors. This code is officially called the "Hex RGB". For a chart of these color codes, try a web search on the terms "hex rgb chart" or see a partial chart at `http://www.w3.org/TR/2001/WD-css3-color-20010305#x11-color`.

Display left menu shows a list of the pages in the lesson. By default, question pages are not shown in this list. However, on each question page, you can select a setting to show that page in the left menu.

Access Control

The settings in this area determine if the lesson is password-protected, and the dates for which the lesson is available.

Password protected lesson and Password require a student to enter the password to access the lesson. Note that if you password-protect a lesson, students can still see it on the course's Home Page. They are prompted to enter the password after they select the lesson. Also note that each student has the same password for the lesson.

Other

Tree view displays a list of the pages and questions in this lesson. This is different from the Display left menu option, which displays only pages and not questions.

Display high scores show a list of the high scores for the lesson. When a student achieves one of the high scores, she or he can choose a name for the score. If this is a practice lesson, the high scores will not display even if this is turned on. Number of high scores displayed limits the number of scores displayed.

Use this lesson's settings as defaults will make the settings you have chosen on this page the defaults for the next lesson that you create.

Visible to users shows this lesson or hides it from users. You can keep the lesson hidden while you work on it.

After you click Save changes, you'll be asked what you want to do next:

- Import questions
- Add a Branch Table
- Add a Question Page here

Question Pages

After you fill out and save the Settings page, you can choose to create the first question page. Even though it's called a "question page", the page can contain more than just a question. It's a web page, so you can add any content to it. Usually, it contains information and a question to test the student's retention. You can choose different types of questions:

- True/false
- Short answer
- Numeric
- Matching
- Essay

In the following example, you can see the question page contains some text, a graphic, and three responses to the question:

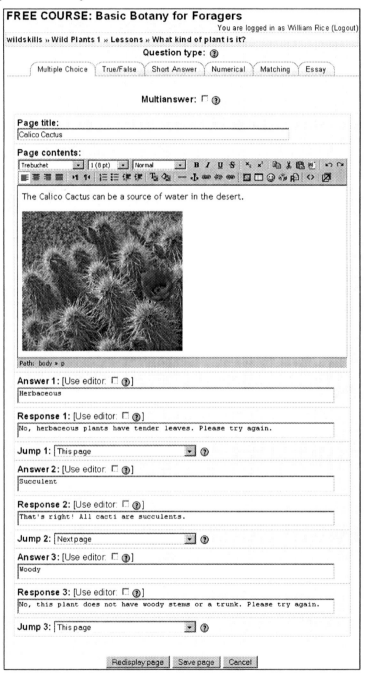

When filling out a question page, Answer 1 is automatically assumed to be the correct answer, so Jump 1 automatically reads Next page. This is because in most cases, you want a correct response to result in the next page in the lesson being displayed. However, you can select any existing page in the lesson for the jump. Note that when you are filling out the first question page, there are no other pages to jump to, so the jumps on the first page will read This page. After creating more pages, you can go back and change the jumps.

The jumps that you create will determine the order in which the pages are presented to the student. For any answer, you can select a jump to the last page of the lesson. The last page displays an end-of-lesson message and, if you choose, the grade for the lesson. It also displays a link that takes the student back to the course's Home Page.

The Flow of Pages

The most common usage of question pages and jumps is to enforce a straight-through lesson structure. A correct answer results in a positive response like "That's correct!" and then jumps to the next page. An incorrect answer results in a negative response or a correction. An incorrect answer can then redisplay the page so the student can try again, as in the example previously. (Jump 1: This page). Or, an incorrect answer can jump to a remedial page. The order of pages the student would follow if (s)he answered every question correctly is called the logical order. This is what the teacher sees when editing the lesson, and displaying all of the pages in the same window.

Question Pages without Questions

You are not required to add a question to a Question page. If you omit the questions, Moodle displays a Continue link that takes the student to the next page. This is useful on remedial pages, where you want to ensure that the student returns to the main lesson flow.

It is also useful if you want to enforce the reading of material in a certain order. Recall that on a course's Home Page, course material can be read in any order. However, using a lesson, you can enforce a given order for the reading of course material. If you want to enforce a particular order for the entire course, you can make the course one big lesson. This is as close as Moodle comes to a commercial learning management system's ability to enforce an order of material on a course.

The View All Pages Link

When editing is turned on, and you select the view all pages link, you see a check lesson page like the one shown in the following screenshot:

The name of the lesson appears at the top of the page. Beneath that are the question pages. The pages display in their logical order. Notice that the pictures do not display, just the text of the pages. The purpose of this screen is not to edit individual questions, but to help you see the flow of the lesson.

Testing the Questions and Navigation

After each question is a Check Question or Check branch table button. Clicking this button shows the question as a student will see it, enabling you to test the interaction. Essentially it starts the lesson at that point. The first question is the first page in the branch, so instead of displaying Check Question it displays Check branch table.

At the bottom of the page is a Check navigation link. Clicking this link takes you to the first page in the lesson, enabling you to test the entire lesson from start to finish.

Editing and Rearranging Questions

In the title bar of each question is an edit icon: ▲. Clicking this takes you to the editing page for that question. To rearrange your questions, click the up/down arrow ↕ for the question you want to move. Note that it is the jumps that determine the order in which Moodle presents the questions. If a question is set to jump to the next page, rearranging the pages can change the jumps. A question can also be set to jump to a specific, named page. In that case the order in which the questions appear on this page doesn't determine the order in which they are presented, so rearranging the questions here doesn't change the way the lesson works.

Adding Questions

At the top of the page, and after each question, is an Add a Question Page here link. Clicking this link takes you to a new question page. When you save the new question, it is added at the link's location. Again, remember that it is the jumps that determine the order in which questions appear, not the order of the questions on this page.

You can also import questions from other learning management systems using the Import Questions link. Clicking this link takes you to a page where you select the format of the questions, and import the question file.

You can also add a cluster of questions. A cluster is a group of questions. One of the questions is displayed when the lesson is run. The question is randomly chosen, so the lesson is a little different each time the student runs it.

Adding a Branch Table and Branch End

A branch table is a page with links to other pages in the lesson. The most common use for a branch table is as a table of contents at the beginning of a lesson.

Each link in a branch table has a description and the title of the page to jump to. You do not need to link to every page in a lesson.

You can use a branch table to divide the lesson into a number of branches (or sections). Each branch can contain a number of pages on the same topic.

You can mark the end of a branch with an End of Branch page. This page returns the student back to the preceding branch table. You can edit this return jump, but most leave it as is. If you do not mark the end of a branch with an End of Branch page, you will proceed out of the branch and to the next question.

Quizzes

Moodle offers a flexible quiz builder. Each question is a full-featured web page that can include any valid HTML code. This means a question can include text, images, sound files, movie files, and anything else you can put on a web page.

In most instructor-led courses, a quiz or test is a major event. Handing out the quizzes, stopping class to take them, and grading them can take a lot of the teacher's time. In Moodle, creating, taking, and grading quizzes is much faster. This means that you can use quizzes liberally throughout your courses. For example, you can:

- Use a short quiz after each reading assignment to ensure the students completed the reading. Shuffle the questions and answers to prevent sharing among the students, and make the quiz available only for the week/month that the students are supposed to complete the reading.

- Use a quiz as a practice test. Allow several attempts, and/or use the Adaptive mode to allow students to attempt a question until they get it right. Then the quiz becomes both practice and learning material.

- Use a quiz as a survey. Ask the students to rate their understanding, satisfaction with the course or instructor, the pace of the course, etc. The score at the end of the quiz is not their grade, but the grade they give to the course.

Quiz Settings

When you first create a quiz, you see the Settings page. The introduction is displayed when a student selects the quiz, as shown in the following screenshot:

🗋 **Updating quiz in topic 3** ⑦

Name:	Leaf Types and Shapes

Introduction:

About the HTML editor ⑦

Leaves are one of the primary ways that field guides identify plants, so understanding the terminology used to describe them is important. Check your understanding with this short quiz.

Open the quiz: 8 ▾ July ▾ 2005 ▾ 16 ▾ 15 ▾ ⑦

Close the quiz: 8 ▾ July ▾ 2006 ▾ 16 ▾ 15 ▾ ⑦

Time limit: None ▾ ⑦

Questions per page: Unlimited ▾ ⑦

Shuffle questions: No ▾ ⑦

Shuffle answers: Yes ▾ ⑦

Attempts allowed: Unlimited attempts ▾ ⑦

Each attempt builds on the last: No ▾ ⑦

Grading method: Highest grade ▾ ⑦

Adaptive mode: No ▾ ⑦

Apply penalties: No ▾ ⑦

Decimal points: 2 ▾ ⑦

Students may review: Responses Scores Feedback Answers ⑦

	Responses	Scores	Feedback	Answers
Immediately after the attempt:	☑	☑	☑	☑
Later, while the quiz is still open:	☐	☐	☐	☐
After the quiz is closed:	☐	☐	☐	☐

Show quiz in a "secure" window: No ▾ ⑦

Require password: ⑦

Require network address: ⑦

Group mode: No groups ▾ ⑦

Visible to students: Show ▾

[Save changes] [Save changes and edit questions] [Cancel]

The Open and Close dates determine when the quiz is available. Note that even if the quiz is closed, it is still shown on the course's Home Page and students might still try to select it. When they do select a closed quiz, the students see a message saying it is closed. If you want to hide a quiz, change the last setting on this page Visible to students.

By default, a quiz does not have a Time limit. If you want to set a time limit, use this setting. When time runs out, the quiz is automatically submitted with the answers that have been filled out. A time limit can help to prevent the use of reference materials while taking the quiz. For example, if you want students to answer the questions from memory, but all the answers are in the course textbook, setting a timer might discourage students from taking the time to look up the answer to each question.

By default, all questions in a quiz display on the same page. Questions per page breaks the quiz up into smaller pages. Moodle inserts the page breaks for you. On the Editing quiz page, you can move these page breaks.

Shuffle questions and Shuffle answers change the order of the questions and answers each time the quiz is displayed. This discourages the sharing of quiz answers among students.

Attempts allowed allows the student to keep trying the quiz. Each attempt builds on the last retains the answers from one attempt to another. Taken together, these two settings can be used to create a quiz that the student can keep trying until (s)he gets it right. This transforms the quiz from a test into a learning tool.

If you allow several attempts, the grading method determines which grade is recorded in the course's gradebook: the Highest, Average, First, or Last grade.

The Adaptive mode allows multiple attempts for each question. This is different from Attempts allowed, which allows multiple attempts at the whole quiz. When you make a quiz adaptive, each question offers you the option to:

- Display a message if the student answered incorrectly, and redisplay the question.
- Display a message if the student answered incorrectly, and then display a different question.

Apply penalties only applies when a quiz is adaptive. For each question the student answers wrongly, points are subtracted from the student's score. You can choose the penalty for each question.

Decimal points apply to the student's grade.

Students may review controls if and when a student can review his/her past attempts at the quiz.

Show quiz in a "secure" window launches the quiz in a new browser window. It uses JavaScript to disable copying, saving, and printing. This security is not foolproof.

If you enter anything into Require password, the student must enter that password to access the quiz.

With Require network address, you can restrict access to the quiz to particular IP address(es). For example:

- 146.203.59.235 permits a single computer to access the quiz. If this computer is acting as a proxy, the other computers "behind" it can also access the quiz.
- 146.203 will permit any IP address starting with those numbers. If those numbers belong to your company, then you effectively limit access to the quiz to your company's campus.
- 146.203.59.235/20 permits a subnet to access the quiz.

Group mode works the same as it does for any other resource (resources were covered in Chapter 4).

Visible to students shows and hides the quiz.

A Word about Security

If you absolutely must give a web-based test that is resistant to cheating, consider these strategies:

- Create a very large number of questions, but have the quiz show only a small set of them. This makes sharing of questions less useful.
- Shuffle the questions and answers. This also makes sharing of questions more difficult.
- Apply a time limit. This makes using reference material more difficult.
- Open the quiz for only a few hours. Have your students schedule the time to take the quiz. Make yourself available during this time to help with technical issues.

Question Categories

Every question belongs to a category. In the screenshot shown overleaf, you can see that the selected category of question is Leaves. To add or rename a question category, click the Edit categories button.

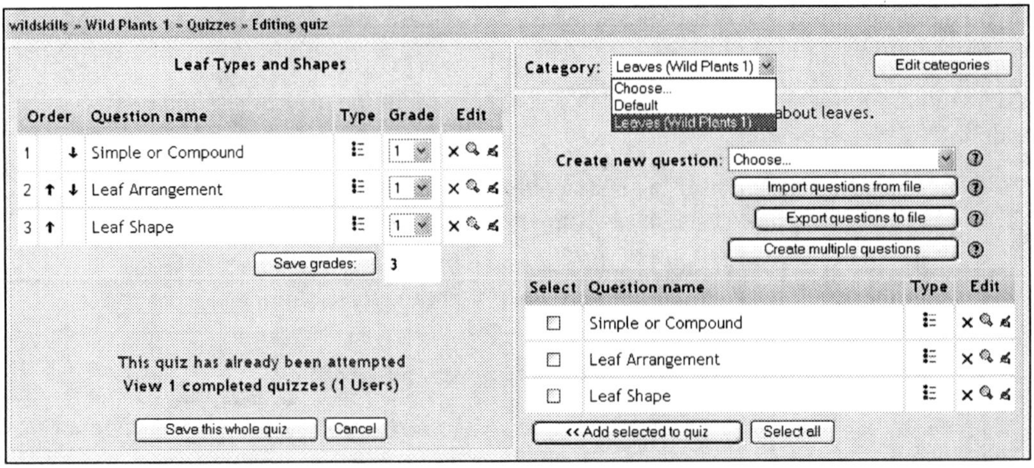

All questions are available to all quizzes. When you make a quiz, you can add any question from any category in your Moodle site.

Managing the Proliferation of Questions and Categories

As the site administrator, you might want to monitor the creation of new question categories to ensure that they are logically named, don't have a lot of overlap, and are appropriate for the purpose of your site. Because these question categories and the questions in them are shared among course creators, they can be a powerful tool for collaboration or a source of confusion and duplication. Consider using the site-wide Teachers forum to notify your teachers and course creators of new questions and categories.

Creating a Question

Under the Create a new question drop-down menu, selecting a question type opens an edit question window. The next section covers the types of questions you can create. But no matter what type of question you choose to create, it will be added to the current category.

Also, every question has a name, as you can see in the screenshot shown above. You should name your questions so that you will remember the content of the question. For example, "Leaf Question 1" would not be a very descriptive name.

If you forget what a question says, you can always click on the 🔍 button next to the question to preview it.

Types of Questions

You can mix different types of questions on the same quiz. In the following screenshot, you can see that the existing three questions are multiple choice and the teacher is about to add a matching question.

Multiple Choice

Multiple choice questions can have a single correct answer or multiple correct answers.

True/False

The student selects from two options: True or False.

Short Answer

The student types a word or phrase into the answer field. This is checked against the correct answer or answers. There may be several correct answers, with different grades.

Numerical

Just as in a short-answer question, the student enters an answer into the answer field. However, the answer to a numerical question can have an acceptable error, which you set when creating the question. For example, you can designate that the correct answer is 5, plus or minus 1. Then, any number from 4 to 6 inclusive will be marked correct.

Calculated

When you create a calculated question, you enter a formula that gets displayed in the text of the question. The formula can contain one or more wildcards, which are replaced with numbers when the quiz is run. Wildcards are enclosed in curly brackets.

For example, if you type the question What is 3 * {a}?, Moodle will replace {a} with a random number. You can also enter wildcards into the answer field, so that the correct answer is 3 * {a}. When the quiz is run, the question will display What is 3 * {a}? and the correct answer will be the calculated value of 3 * {a}.

Matching

After you create a matching question, you then create a list of subquestions, and enter the correct answer for each subquestion. The student must match the correct answer with each question. Each subquestion receives equal weight for scoring the question.

Description

This is not a question. It displays whatever web content you enter. When you add a description question, Moodle gives you the same editing screen as when you create a web page.

Random Short-Answer Matching

Recall that a matching question consists of subquestions and answers that must be matched to each subquestion. When you select Random Short-Answer Matching, Moodle draws random short-answer questions from the current category. It then uses those short-answer questions, and their answers, to create a matching question.

To the student, this looks just like any other matching question. The difference is that the subquestions were drawn at random from short-answer questions in the current category.

Random

When this type of question is added to a quiz, Moodle draws a question at random from the current category. The question is drawn at the time the student takes the quiz.

Embedded Answers

An embedded answers question consists of a passage of text, with answers inserted into the text. Multiple-choice, fill-in-the-blank, and numeric answers can be inserted into the question. Moodle's help file gives the following example:

3
 	
8 Marks
	This question consists of some text with an answer embedded right here [_____ ▼] and right after that you will have to deal with this short answer [_____] and finally we have a floating point number [_____] .
	
	Note that addresses like www.moodle.org and smileys ☺ all work as normal:
	a) How good is this? [___ ▼]
	b) What grade would ▮▮▮▮ve it? [_____]
	           Yes
	           No
	
	Good luck!

Notice that the question presents a drop-down list first, which is essentially a multiple-choice question. Then, it presents a short answer (fill-in-the-blank) question, followed by a numeric question. Finally, there's another multiple-choice question (the Yes/No drop-down) and another numeric question.

There is no graphical interface to create embedded answers questions. You need to use a special format that is explained in the help files.

SCORM

SCORM stands for **Sharable Content Object Reference Model**. SCROM is a standard, not a product or feature. It is a collection of specifications that enable learning management systems to use content developed for each other.

The SCORM module allows you to upload any standard SCORM package to include in your course:

The Summary is displayed when the student selects this activity from the course's Home Page.

To select the SCORM package that you want to import, use Course package and the Choose button

If the package you imported is graded, select one of the Grading methods.

If Auto-continue is set to Yes, when the student finishes with one Sharable Content Object, the next one in the course displays automatically. Otherwise, the student must click a Continue button to proceed.

Enable preview mode enables the student to browse the content without taking the associated test. The content is marked as browsed.

Because Sharable Content Objects display in a separate window, you can set the window Width and Height for them.

Survey

Moodle's survey consists of questions about the students' attitudes towards learning in general and the course specifically, and about the students' experience with the course. Moodle enables you to create five different surveys, all of which are pre-created for you. The survey questions are designed to help you assess your students. The questions and choices in these surveys are set, and you cannot edit them. If the stock survey questions are not appropriate for your usage, you will need to repurpose a quiz into a survey.

Creating a Survey

To create a survey, add it to your activity and then select the Survey type. Set the Group mode, edit the introductory text, and the survey is complete. The questions are set for you.

Survey Types

Moodle offers five different surveys, divided into three survey types.

COLLES

COLLES stands for **Constructivist On-Line Learning Environment Survey**. There are three surveys in this category. Each consists of 24 statements, for which the student indicates a level of agreement or disagreement. The questions ask about:

- The course's relevance to the student's interests and professional goals
- The level of critical or reflective thinking that the student applies to the material in the course
- The level of interactivity the student engages in during the course
- The level of tutor support the student is receiving in the course

- The level of peer support the student is receiving in the course
- The success of the students' tutor's, and other students' interpretation of the interaction between them

The three COLLES surveys ask students about their preferred learning environment, the actual learning environment they are experiencing in the course, and a combination of the two.

Survey type:	Choose... ▼
	Choose...
	ATTLS (20 item version)
	Critical Incidents
	COLLES (Actual)
	COLLES (Preferred and Actual)
	COLLES (Preferred)

ATTLS

ATTLS stands for **Attitudes To Thinking and Learning Survey**. It consists of 20 questions that ask about the student's style of learning, discussion, and debate. For example, the survey asks about the student's attitude towards logic versus personal concerns:

> I value the use of logic and reason over the incorporation of my own concerns when solving problems.

The ATTLS questions are useful for measuring the student's attitudes in general, but not for measuring the student's perception of or satisfaction with a course.

Critical Incidents

The Critical Incidents survey is different from the COLLES and ATTLS surveys in two ways:

- It is much shorter; only five questions.
- Students answer by typing short responses instead of selecting from multiple choices.

This survey asks students how they feel about recent events in the course. The five questions in the Critical Incidents survey are:

1. At what moment in class were you most engaged as a learner?
2. At what moment in class were you most distanced as a learner?
3. What action from anyone in the forums did you find most affirming or helpful?
4. What action from anyone in the forums did you find most puzzling or confusing?
5. What event surprised you most?

When to Use the Different Types of Surveys

At the beginning of a course, the COLLES (Preferred) survey can give you an idea of the students' preferred way of learning. This can help you to design and present the course in the best way for your students. During the course, you can use a COLLES (Actual) survey to measure how well the course is meeting their needs. These are long surveys, so use them sparingly.

The ATTLS survey can also be used at the beginning of a course to help you understand the students' learning style. Remember that this survey is about the student, not the course. You might want to ask each new student in your learning site to complete an ATTLS survey before participating in any courses. Then each teacher can check their students' ATTLS surveys, and know "who they are dealing with" in their course.

Because the Critical Incidents survey is short, and asks about recent events, you can use this survey after each topic or week. It provides a useful guide for making quick, small changes to a course in progress.

Summary

Moodle's assignments, journals, and lessons enable you to create course material that students interact with. This interaction is more engaging, and usually more effective, than courses consisting of static material that the students view. While you will probably begin creating your course by adding static material, the next step should usually be to ask, "How can I add interactivity to this course?" Lessons can even take the place of many static web pages, since they consist of web pages with a question at the end of each page.

Survey and Choice give teachers the opportunity to assess students, their attitudes towards learning, and their satisfaction with a course. The ATTLS survey can become part of student's record, available to all teachers who have that student in a course. The COLLES (Preferred) survey can be used at the beginning of a course to assess the student's motivation and expectations, while the COLLES (Actual) can be used every few weeks to assess student satisfaction. Add a Critical Incidents survey after each topic or week, and a Choice as needed, and the result is a structured, ongoing conversation between the students and teacher.

6

Adding Social Course Material

Social course activities encourage student-to-student interaction. Peer interaction is one of the most powerful learning tools that Moodle offers. It not only encourages learning, but also exploration. It also makes courses more interesting, which increases student participation and satisfaction. This chapter teaches you how to add social resources to a course, and how to make best use of them.

Chat

The Chat module creates a chat room where students can have real-time, online chats.

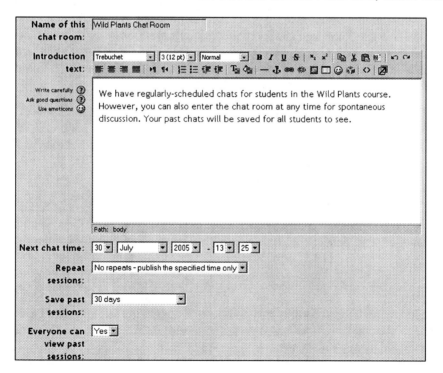

When you add a chat room to a course, any student in the course can enter that chat room at any time. The chat room can become a meeting place for the students in the course, where they can come to collaborate on work and exchange information. If you give group assignments, or have students rate other students' assignments, consider adding a chat room to the course and encouraging students to use it.

Chat Security

The only security for a chat room is turning the group mode on, so that only students in a selected group can enter.

Remember that in the Course Settings page, you can set the Enrolment duration as Unlimited. This means that once a student is enrolled in the course, she or he is always enrolled until you manually unenroll the student. If you leave the course open to all students who were ever enrolled, consider segregating your chat by groups. Then, create a group that includes only the currently enrolled students. This prevents previous students from giving away too much in the chat room.

Chat Times

The chat settings page enables you to set a time for the next chat, and to set recurring chat times. These times are listed in the Calendar and Upcoming Events blocks. Note that chat is not restricted to these times; they are only announced as a way for people in the course to "make a date" for the chat. Spontaneous chats have the best chance of happening if the course has a lot of students who frequent the course's Home Page. Also, consider adding the Online Users block, so that when students visit the site they will know who is online and can invite others into the chat room.

To make the chat room available only during designated times, you should make the person running the chat a course creator. Then, hide the chat room during off hours. When the chat is about to begin, the course creator can show the chat room.

Archiving Chats

Past chats are saved. The Save past sessions setting enables you to set a time limit for saving chats. The setting for Everyone can view past sessions determines whether students can view past chats (Yes) or whether only teachers can view past chats (No).

Forum

You can add any number of forums to a course, and also to the site's Front Page. Anyone with access to the course will have access to the forums. You can use group mode to limit access to a forum to specific groups.

When a student enters a forum, the student sees the description entered during creation of the forum, as shown in the above figure.

While writing a forum posting, the student uses the same online, WYSIWYG editor you see when creating web pages in Moodle. Also, you can allow students to upload files into a forum. If you ask students to collaborate on assignments, or ask them to review each others' work, consider adding a forum specifically for discussing the assignment. Encourage the students to use the forum to preview each others' work and collaborate on the assignments.

Discussion Equals Topic

In the Moodle forum, discussions are the equivalent of topics or threads. When the setting for Can a student post to this forum? is set to Discussions and replies are allowed, students can create new topics and reply to existing topics. When set to No discussions, but replies are allowed, students can post to existing topics, but the teacher must create discussion topics. When set to No discussions, no replies, only the teacher can create discussions or post replies.

Using a Forum to Send Mass Emails

The last option, No discussions, no replies, is commonly used when you want to send mass emails to an entire class. Moodle does not have a module just for sending email announcements. So when you want to send an email to everyone in a class (or in your site), you can create a Forum for the class (or site), select Yes for Force everyone to be subscribed? and then hide the Forum from view. With the Forum hidden, only teachers can see it and post messages. When the teacher posts a message, everyone who is subscribed to the Forum receives the message via email. With everyone subscribed, the entire class will receive a copy of each posting by email.

Multiple Forums

Remember that a class can have as many Forums as you want. If your course uses groups, you can designate a different Forum for each group. Also, you can hide old Forums and create new ones. This is useful if you run students through a course on a schedule. Just turning off the old Forums and creating new ones enables you to refresh part of the course.

Glossary

The Glossary activity is one of the most underrated in Moodle. This activity allows participants to create and maintain a list of definitions, like a dictionary. On the surface, a glossary is a list of words and definitions that students can access. However, a course creator can allow students to add to a Glossary. This transforms the glossary from a static listing of vocabulary words to a collaborative tool for learning.

Adding Glossary Entries

Selecting Glossary from the course menu displays the Glossary window. In this window, you can edit and browse the Glossary. The following screenshot shows the Add a new entry tab:

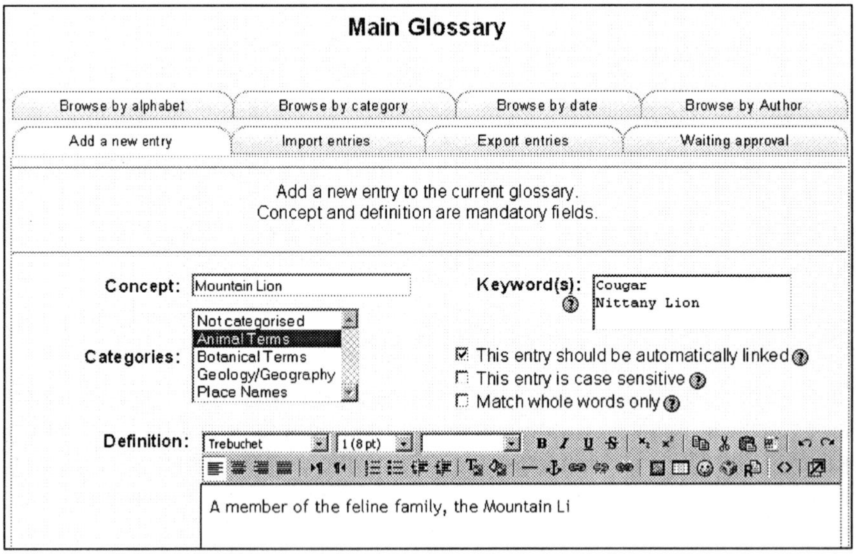

In this tab, Concept is the term that you are adding to the Glossary. Keyword(s) are synonyms, the equivalent of a "see also" in an index or dictionary. These terms will link to the same definition as the concept.

Create new Glossary categories under the Browse by category tab. This is not entirely intuitive; and many users would look for the function to add categories in this window instead. If you allow users to add categories to a glossary, consider pointing this out to them.

You can also upload an optional file for each Glossary entry. The upload button is below the definition (off of our screenshot). This is useful for including a picture in a term's definition. Also, note that the editing window enables you to include hyperlinks in the definition (the 🔗 icon). This can be used to link to freely available information on the Web, such as http://www.wikipedia.org/.

The Import and Export tabs enable you to exchange glossaries between courses and even Moodle installations. You might want to begin a course with a small glossary, and let students add to it as they discover new concepts. If you do this, export the beginning glossary so that you have it available for the next course. The next time you teach the course, you can choose to export everything in the completed course except student information and the glossary. In the new copy, just create a new, blank Glossary and import the starting Glossary.

When you create a Glossary, in the settings window you choose whether terms that students add are approved automatically, or whether they need the teacher's approval. In this example, the Waiting approval tab is unavailable because terms are automatically approved. If that setting were turned off, new terms would await the teacher's approval before being added.

Global versus Local Glossary

When a word from a Glossary appears in the course, it is highlighted in gray. Clicking the word brings up a pop-up window with the word's Glossary entry. By default, a glossary applies only to the course in which it resides. However, you can choose to make a glossary global, in which case the words from that glossary will be highlighted and clickable wherever they are in your site. The work done in one course then becomes available to all the courses on your site. If your site's subject matter is highly focused (as in our example, Wilderness Skills), consider using a global glossary. If your site's subject matter is very broad, as in a university-wide learning site, you should use local glossaries to avoid confusion. For example, imagine you have a course on chemistry and another on statistics. Both use the word "granular," but chemistry uses it to indicate a powdered substance while statistics uses it to indicate a fine level of detail.

Main and Secondary Glossaries

If you want students to be able to add entries to a Glossary, you must make it a Secondary glossary. Only teachers can add terms to a Main glossary. A Secondary glossary has only the terms that the students and teacher add to it. A Main glossary has the terms that the students and teacher added, plus it automatically imports the terms from all of the secondary glossaries in the course.

You can add a Secondary glossary for each section in a course. For example, put a Secondary glossary into each topic or week. Then, you can create a Main glossary for the course that will automatically include all of the terms added to each Secondary glossary. Put the Main glossary into Topic 0, the section at the top of the course's Home Page.

If you want the course to have only one glossary, and you want students to be able to add to it, make it a Secondary glossary. Even though the term "Secondary" implies that there is also a primary or main glossary, this is not the case. You can have just a Secondary glossary (or more than one) in a course, without a Main glossary.

Wiki

The Moodle Wiki module enables students to collaborate on a book-like writing project. Because a Wiki is easy to use, interactive, and organized by date, it encourages informal discussion among the participants. This makes it a powerful tool for recording the thoughts and progress of the students. Old versions of a Wiki are never deleted and can be restored. Wikis can also be searched, just like other course material.

Using Wiki Type and Group Mode to Determine Who Can Edit a Wiki

A Wiki can be open to editing by the entire class, a group, the teacher, or a single student. It can also be open to viewing by the entire class, a group, the teacher, or single student. The course creator determines who can edit the Wiki, and who can see it. This is done using the Type drop-down box and the Groups mode. For a matrix that explains all the options, select the ⊚ icon next to the Type drop-down box.

Making a Wiki editable by only a single student appears to turn the Wiki into a personal journal. However, the difference between a single-student Wiki and a journal is that a journal can be seen only by the student and teacher. A single-student Wiki can be opened for viewing by the entire class, or by the student's group.

Wiki Markup versus HTML Mode

The HTML Mode setting determines whether Wiki authors use standard Wiki markup or HTML code when editing. If you're using the HTML editor for other student activities, setting this to HTML only can simplify this activity for your students. They will get the familiar HTML editor, and don't need to learn the Wiki markup language. However, if your students are accustomed to Wikis, you may want to select No HTML. This enables them to use Wiki markup, which is faster for experienced typists.

Enabling the Uploading of Binary Files

Allow binary files enables or disables the ability to upload non-text files to the Wiki. The most common usage of binary files are pictures embedded on the Wiki pages, or attached to the Wiki. Setting to Yes permits both. The size of the uploaded files is limited by the setting maxbytes in the Variables page.

When to Use CamelCase Linking

CamelCase is the practice of writing compound words or phrases where the words are joined without spaces, and each word is capitalized within the compound. This is also known as **Bicapitalization**, **InterCaps**, and **MixedCase**. CamelCase is a standard identifier naming convention for several programming languages, and carried over into the standard wiki markup language. It is also fashionable in marketing for names of products and companies.

The original Wiki, **WikiWiki**, the convention for creating hyperlinks was CamelCase. However, because of problems with that syntax, some Wikis (such as Wikipedia) switched to an alternative syntax that allowed any sequence of characters to be a link. If you're going to import older Wikis into a Moodle Wiki, you might want to enable CamelCase so that the older Wiki's links import correctly. However, if you're not importing an older Wiki, it is best to disable CamelCase because its usage has fallen into disfavor.

Student Admin Options

The Student Admin Options become available to students only if students are allowed to edit the Wiki. If you enable these, but do not allow students to edit the Wiki, they will have no effect.

Page Name and Initial Page

Notice that in the example shown previously, the name of the Wiki is the rather uninspired "Group Wiki". If you leave the Page Name and Initial Page fields blank, the name on the first page of the Wiki will be taken from the name field. To override that, you can enter a page name in the Page Name field, or, set the initial page of the Wiki to any other web page.

Workshop

A workshop provides a place for the students in a class to see an example project, upload their individual projects, and see and assess each other's projects. When a teacher requires each student to assess the work of several other students, the workshop becomes a powerful collaborative grading tool.

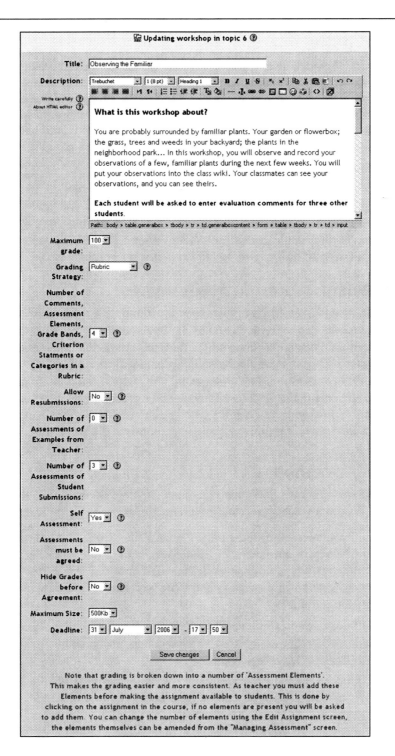

Workshop Strategies

Workshops can be ungraded, peer graded, instructor graded, or a combination of peer and instructor graded. Workshops enable you to create very specific assessment criteria for the graders to use. Also, workshops let you set due dates for submitting work, and for grading work. You can use these and other features to build a strategy for making best use of workshops in your courses.

Peer Assessment of Assignments

One strategy for workshops is to have students assess each other's work, before submitting that same work as a graded assignment. For example, you could create a workshop where students assess each other's subject matter, outlines, and hypothesis for their term papers. Or they could assess each other's photos for specific technical and artistic criteria before submitting them to the instructor for grading.

Timing of Submissions and Assessments

Workshops enable you to set different due dates for submitting work, and for assessing other student's work. If you set both due dates the same, so many students might submit their work just before the submission deadline that they cannot all be assessed before the assessment deadline. Consider setting the submission deadline well before the assessment deadline. Then, before opening up the assessment ability to the students, examine the work submitted and ensure that it's close to what you expected or were trying to elicit from the students. You might even want to use the time between submission and assessment to refine your assessment criteria, in response to the work submitted.

Creating a Workshop

The fields in the workshop window give you many choices. No matter what you enter into each field, your many decisions can be summed up as:

- What will you have each student do? Create a file offline and upload it to the workshop? Write a journal entry? Participate in an online chat? Perform some offline activity and report on it via email or Wiki? While the workshop window enables the student to upload a file, you can also require any other activity from the student.

- Who will assess the assignments? Will the teacher assess all assignments? Will students be required to assess other students' assignments? Will each student self-assess his or her work?

- How will the assignments be assessed? You can determine the number of criteria upon which each assignment is assessed, the grading scale, and the type of grading.

- When will students be allowed to submit their assignments? The assignment becomes available as soon as you show it. However, you can require students to assess an example before being allowed to submit their own work, and you also set a deadline for submitting.

All of the fields that we cover below are variations of these questions. The online help does a good job of explaining how to use each field. Instead of repeating how to use each field here, we will focus on how your choices affect the student and teacher experience.

Workshop Fields

The workshop activity is the most complex tool currently available in Moodle. Workshops are designed so that a student's work can be submitted and offered for peer review within a structured framework. Workshops provide a process for both instructor and peer feedback on open-ended assignments, such as essays and research papers. There are easy-to-use interfaces for uploading assignments, performing self-assessments, and peer reviews of other students' papers. The key to the workshop is the scoring guide, which is a set of specific criteria for making judgments about the quality of a given work. There are several fields under workshop. They will be explained in the following sections. They provide a place for the students in the class as well as the teachers to make the best use of Moodle.

Title and Description

Your students will see and click on the Title. The Description should give instructions for completing the workshop. If you want to make printer-friendly instructions, you can upload a .pdf file to the course files area, and put a link to the document in the workshop description.

Grade for Assessments and Grade for Submission

Added together, these two fields determine the maximum points a student can earn for a workshop. Grade for assessments is the maximum number of points a student can be given by the grader(s), whether it's the teacher or other students who are assigning the grade. Grade for submission is points the student gets just for submitting the work. If you choose Not Graded for the Grading Strategy, these grades are irrelevant.

The assessment grade can come from the teacher or other students. If the field Number of Assessments of Student Submissions is set to something greater than zero, then students assess each other's work. If it's set to zero, then only the teacher is assessing work.

Making the maximum grade a multiple of the number of assessment elements enables the students to more easily interpret their grades. For example, suppose a workshop will be assessed on five elements. For each element, the assessor will choose from four statements:

1. The workshop does not meet this requirement in any way.
2. The workshop partially meets this requirement.
3. The workshop meets this requirement.
4. The workshop exceeds this requirement.

You could assign a point value of zero for each 1, one point for each 2, two points for each 3, and three points for each 4. Then, each element would be worth a maximum of three points. With five elements, the workshop would have a maximum grade of 15. This would make it easy for the student to interpret his or her grade.

Grading Strategy

A workshop assignment is quite flexible in the type of grading scheme used. It can be:

Accumulative

In the Accumulative grading strategy, the grade for each element is added to arrive at the accumulated grade. This style of grading enables you to present the reviewer with a numeric scale. You can also present the reviewer with Yes or No questions, such as "Does this workshop meet the requirement?" Or, you can present the reviewer with a grading scale, such as "Poor, Fair, Good, Excellent". If you do use a Yes or No or a grading scale, you will assign a point value to each response. Consider informing the reviewer of the value of each response. For example, instead of just writing:

- Poor
- Fair
- Good
- Excellent

Consider writing:

- Poor (1 point)
- Fair (2 points)
- Good (3 points)
- Excellent (4 points)

Not Graded

When this is selected, students can comment upon each assessment element but do not select a grade. The teacher can grade students' comments. In that case, the workshop is transformed from one where students grade each other to where the teacher grades each student's comments.

This may be especially useful when you want to have a structured discussion about material that you present to the students. As the course creator, you can present the students with material uploaded to the workshop, or use the workshop's description to direct the students to material they must assess. After the students view the material, they enter the workshop and leave comments according to the elements presented. Because the workshop presents the students with evaluation elements, and it requires that they complete each element, your discussion is more structured than if you use a Wiki or journal.

Error Banded

When you choose this option, students evaluate a workshop using a series of Yes or No questions. Usually, you create questions to evaluate whether the workshop met a requirement, such as "Does the student present a variety of opinions?"

When writing an error banded question, make sure that it can be answered using only Yes or No. A sign that you need to revise your question is the presence of the word "or". For example, don't write "Did the student describe the plant well enough to distinguish it from others, or, is there still doubt as to which plant the student is describing?" Such a question cannot be answered Yes or No.

Making Best Use of Error Banded Questions

The answer to an error banded question is sometimes very clear, and sometimes subjective. For example, the question "Did the student describe the plant well enough to distinguish it from others?" is subjective. One reviewer might think the student did an adequate job of describing the plant, while another might think otherwise. Error banded questions can be a good way to perform subjective peer evaluations of each student's work.

If the work requires a more objective evaluation, such as "Did the student include all five identifying features covered in this lesson?" you may not need a workshop. That kind of objective evaluation can be easily performed by the teacher using an assignment.

Criterion and Rubric

For a criterion grading scale, write several statements that apply to the project. Each statement has a grade assigned to it. The reviewers choose the one statement that best describes the project. This single choice completes the review. The rubric grading scale is the same as criterion, except reviewers choose a statement for multiple criteria. Overleaf is a screenshot of an assessment element:

Assessment by William Rice	
Friday, April 20 2007, 02:20 PM	
Element 1:	Please comment on the variety of plants chosen by this student.
	Weight: 2.0
Select	**Criterion**
⦿	No variety.
○	A good variety of plants.
○	Outstanding variety.
Feedback:	[ ]
Add Comment	

For a rubric, you would create several of these elements, and the reviewers would select a statement for each of them. For a criterion scale, you would create only one of these.

Number of Comments, Assessment Elements, Grade Bands, Criterion Statements, or Categories in Rubric

This field determines how many elements will be evaluated. No matter what number you select, the reviewers will always be presented with a general comments field into which they can type text. If you set this field to zero, reviewers will see only the general comments field.

Allow Resubmissions

The name of this field implies that a student can replace a previous submission with a new one. Actually, if you turn this option on, students can submit more than once but all previous submissions are retained. Also, the latest submissions are not any more likely to be evaluated than earlier submissions. Each submission is equally likely to be assigned to a reviewer.

This has implications for course management. For example, suppose for the field Number of Assessments of Student Submissions, you select 3. Partway through the course, you run a report showing that most students have completed their three assessments (they have evaluated three other students' work). Then, students begin resubmitting their work. These resubmissions will be distributed, at random, among the reviewers who have assessments left. As course manager, you need to determine if there are enough assessments left to cover the resubmissions.

The system keeps the highest grade of all the assignments submitted by the student (the highest grade is the largest teacher-peer combined score).

Number of Assessments of Examples from Teacher

Setting this field to a number greater than zero forces the students to assess that number of example projects from the teacher. The student must comment upon and grade the example. The student's assessment can be graded by the teacher. The student cannot submit her or his work until she or he has gone through the example the teacher provided.

As a teacher, you may want to require students to view an example before submitting their work, without grading them on their assessments. Setting the Number of Comments field to zero for the example will prevent the students from having to evaluate the work. You as the teacher can verify that they have viewed the example, without needing to grade them.

Comparison of Assessments

Work is often assessed by both the teacher and students. The work being assessed can be examples provided by the teacher or work submitted by the students. In either case, it can be assessed by both teacher and student.

When a student assesses a piece of work, the assessment can be graded. For example, suppose the teacher is conducting an online digital photography class. The teacher supplies a photo and asks students to rate the photo's contrast, brightness, focus, etc. The students can be graded on their assessments. (Did they notice the overexposed area on the subject's cheek? Did they notice the eyes were a little out of focus?) Moodle grades a student's assessment by comparing it to the teacher's assessment of the same work. The closer the student's assessment agrees with the one given by the teacher, the more points the student earns.

How close to the teacher's assessment must the student's be to earn a good grade? That is determined by this setting. When Fair is selected, random guessing will usually give a score of zero, or close to zero. The other settings range from Very Lax to Very Strict. You can change this setting on the fly, and evaluate its effect on student grades.

Number of Assessments of Student Submissions

This field determines how many other projects each student is asked to review. If there are more submissions than the allowed assessments, the reviewer will get only the number set in this field. Some projects will not be reviewed.

Weight for Teacher Assessments

This value can range from zero to ten. If set to zero, the teacher's assessment for a piece of work carries no weight for the student's grade. If set to 1, the teacher's assessment carries the same weight as a student's assessment of that piece of work. If set to 2, the teacher's assessment counts as much as two student assessments, and so on. If students have consistently over or under-graded assignments in a workshop, this setting can be used by the teacher to raise or lower the overall grades.

Over Allocation

As students submit or upload their work to a workshop, Moodle allocates it to other students for assessment. The field Number of Assessments of Student Submissions determines how many submissions each student is required to assess. Ideally, everyone will submit their assignments on time, and the students will have plenty of time to evaluate each other's work. For example, suppose there are ten students in the class, and Number of Assessments of Student Submissions is set to 3. That means each of the ten submissions is assessed three times. Moodle assigns the assessments as the work is submitted.

However, if a student submits work late, the students who are going to evaluate the late person's work will need to wait before they can complete their assessments. Let's suppose one student doesn't submit his or her work by the deadline. That means the class is three assessments short. Because Moodle assigns the assessments evenly, this means that three students will end the class one assessment short. Shall we penalize these students for not completing the required three assessments?

In our example, Over Allocation is set to zero, and each submission is evaluated three and only three times. If we set Over Allocation to one, then when the deadline arrives, Moodle will over allocate some work to the students who still need to complete their assessments. In this example, Moodle will randomly choose three pieces of work that have already been assessed three times, and assign them to the three students who are missing an assessment. These pieces of work will then be over allocated by one assessment each. Moodle allows a maximum over allocation of two.

Self Assessment

If this is set to Yes, each student is asked to evaluate his or her own work. This is in addition to the number of student submissions that the student is asked to evaluate.

Assessments must be Agreed

If this is set to Yes, then an assessment made by one student can be viewed by the other reviewers of the same work. If the other reviewers disagree, the evaluation process continues until they agree or until the assignment's closing time is passed. This can be a useful tool for determining how clear your evaluation elements are. If there is a lot of disagreement among reviewers of the same work, revisit your evaluation elements and the instructions you gave the reviewers.

Hide Grades before Agreement

If this is set to Yes, the numeric parts of a project's evaluation are hidden from other reviewers. The reviewers can see each other's comments, but not the grades they've assigned. The grades will appear after the reviewers agree with each other.

League Table of Submitted Work

This creates a list of the best-rated assignments in this workshop. If it is set to zero, no list is created.

Hide Names from Students

When set to Yes, this hides the names of the students whose work is being evaluated. Note that the names of students are never hidden from the teacher. Also, if a teacher assesses a student's work, the teacher cannot do so anonymously. This only hides the names of students who submitted work from the students who are evaluating the work.

Use Password and Password

You can use these fields to password-protect the assignment.

Maximum Size

This field sets the size limit for project files uploaded to the workshop.

Start and End of Submissions/Assessments

These fields determine when the workshop opens and closes. On the closing date, students can no longer upload files, if any hidden grades appear, and students can no longer evaluate others' work.

Release Teacher Grades

You can use this field to withhold the teacher's assessments until a given date.

Group Mode

Just as in other activities, this determines if access is segregated by group.

Visible to Students

This field shows the workshop or hides it from students.

Summary

Moodle offers several options for student-to-student and student-to-teacher interaction. When deciding which social activities to use, consider the level of structure and amount of student-to-student/student-to-teacher interaction you want. For example, chats and Wikis offer a relatively unstructured environment, with lots of opportunity for student-to-student interaction. They are good ways of relinquishing some control of the class to the students. A forum offers more structure because entries are classified by topic. It can be moderated by the teacher, making it even more structured. A workshop offers the most structure, by virtue of the set assessment criteria that students must use when evaluating each other's work. Note that as the activities become more structured, the opportunity for students to get to know one another decreases.

You may want to introduce a chat and/or forum at the beginning of a course, to build "esprit de corps" among the students, then move into a collaborative Wiki, such as a group writing project. Finally, after the students have learned more about each other and are comfortable working together, you might use a workshop for their final project.

7

Welcoming Your Students

Your courses are built and you are ready to go. When prospective students come to your site, what will they see? Will it be a welcome page, with some explanation of your site? Sample courses that are open to the public? A secure Login Page? Each of these is possible, by itself and in combination. In this chapter, you'll determine what kind of welcome page that prospective and existing students receive.

First Impression: Login Page, Front Page, or Your Page?

In Chapter 2, you learned that the site variable Forcelogin can be used to force users to log in to your site. If this is set to Yes, all users see the Login Page as soon as they hit your learning site.

The Login Page does not present much of a welcome for prospective students. It is not a very good sales tool for your site. If you want to welcome prospective students with more information about your learning site, consider using the Front Page or a page of your own design as the welcome page to your site. To do this, you only need to set Forcelogin to No. Then, when people hit your site, they will automatically see the Front Page:

Another alternative is to use your own web page as the Front Page to your site. This page can be your sales pitch, and contain a link to the Front Page or Login Page of your Moodle site. If you select this option, you need to know how your web hosting service handles *.htm and *.php pages.

By default, when a user hits an Apache web server's directory, the server displays the page `index.html` or `index.htm` if it's present in the directory. If neither of those is present, the server displays `index.php`. Moodle's Front Page is `index.php`. This behavior is controlled by a line in the Apache server's configuration file. Here's a default configuration for the Apache version 2.0 web server:

```
DirectoryIndex index.html index.htm index.php index.php4 index.php3
index.cgi index.pl index.html.var index.phtml
```

This means that if you put a file called `index.html` in Moodle's directory, when visitors come to your Moodle site they will see `index.html` instead of Moodle's Front Page (which is `index.php`). This enables you to construct exactly the welcome page you want, unconstrained by Moodle's Front Page or Login Page layout. From the welcome page, you can put a link to Moodle's Front Page (`index.php`). You can test this behavior by putting `index.html` in your Moodle directory and hitting that directory with your web

176

browser. If `index.html` doesn't display, talk to your webmaster about modifying the directory index line to put `index.html` before `index.php`.

You might want the colors on `index.html` to match those used in your Moodle site. You can see which colors your Moodle site uses by looking in `/theme/themename/config.php`, where `themename` is the name of the theme you're using.

Customizing the Login Page

Moodle's Login Page displays directions for creating a new user account in the right column:

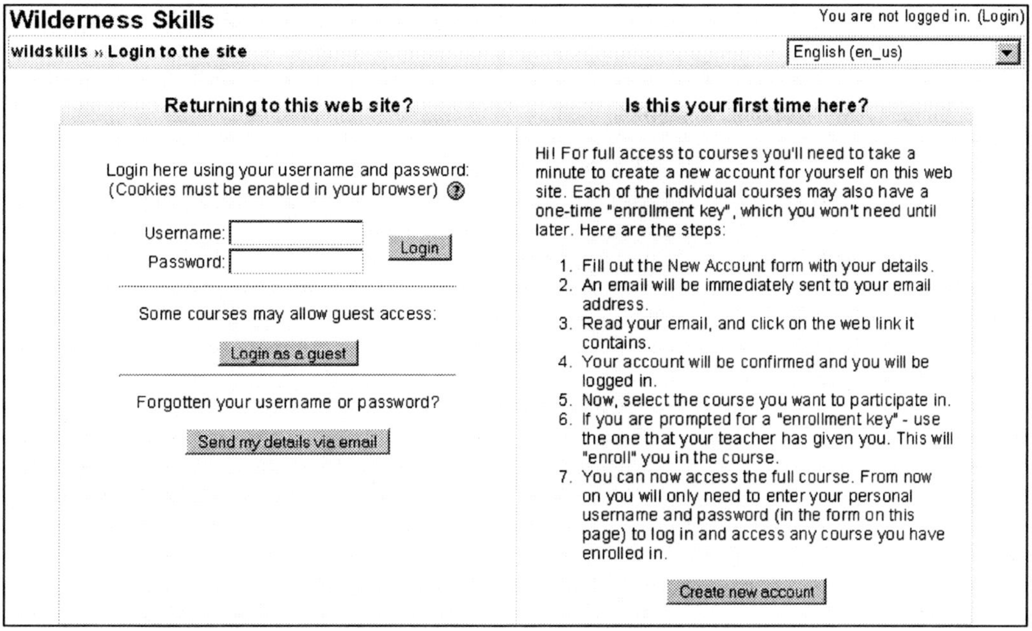

None of Moodle's configuration pages offer you the option to customize those directions. However, you can customize them by editing the language file that you are using for your site.

In Chapter 2, during the installation, you learned that Moodle stores almost all of its text messages in language files. Each language has a separate directory, such as `\moodle\lang\en` for British English and `\moodle\lang\es` for Spanish (Español). In the screenshot shown previously, the user has selected the language U.S. English, so Moodle will use the text files found in `\moodle\lang\en_us`.

The `moodle.php` file holds the text displayed in the right column. Search `moodle.php` for the line that begins `$string['loginsteps'] =`. This line holds the HTML code displayed in the right column of the Login Page. By editing this line, you can put whatever HTML code you want in that column.

This section covers features that help you control access to your Moodle site. We'll discuss securing courses against anonymous users, opening courses to anonymous users, and when you would want to combine the techniques.

Customizing the Front Page

The Front Page of your Moodle site can do two things. It can do either or both of these:

- Display a list of courses and/or course categories, enabling visitors to jump to a selected course or category.

- Act as a course in itself, by displaying anything that a course can display.

Anything that can be added to a course can be added to the Front Page, so that the Front Page can become its own course. In the following example the Front Page does both of these:

Desert Plants Course Added is a label in Section 1 of the Front Page, as is the text below it. The link below that is a quiz that was added to this section.

Available Courses is the result of choosing to display course categories on the Front Page. This is done with the Front Page format variable on the Site settings page. For more about this, see Chapter 2.

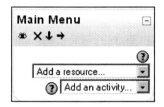

Notice the upper left block displays the title How to Use this Site. In the default installation, this was labeled Main Menu, because it is the Main Menu block. You can add anything to the Main Menu block that you can add to a course.

In my course, we added three web pages using the Add a resource drop-down menu. We also edited the title of the block. In the /lang/en/moodle.php file, the line $string['mainmenu'] = 'Main Menu'; was changed to $string['mainmenu'] = 'How to Use this Site'.

Front Page Blocks

In Chapter 3, you saw how blocks can be added to a course to enhance the user experience. Any block that can be added to a course can also be added to the Front Page. Some blocks behave slightly different when they appear on the Front Page. Other blocks can be added only to the Front Page; they cannot appear in courses. Each subsection below talks about how to add a standard block to the Front Page, and how to make best use of that block.

Activities

The Activities block lists all of the types of activities available in the Front Page. If the type of activity is not used on the Front Page, the link for that type of activity is not presented. When this block is on the site's Front Page, clicking on a type of activity gives a list for the activities on the Front Page (not for the entire site!). In the following screenshot, clicking Resources will display a list of all the static course material that has been added to the Front Page.

Keep in mind that the people taking your Front Page course might be first-time users. That is, the Front Page might be the first Moodle course your visitor has ever taken. The Activities block is not entirely intuitive for a first-time user. One reason is because it uses terminology that is specific to Moodle, such as assignments, choices, lessons, and resources. At this point, your visitor doesn't know what these things are. Another reason the Activities block may be confusing to a first-timer is because it probably lists the activities out of order. The activities are listed in alphabetical order, no matter what order they appear on the Front Page. Moodle encourages exploration, and only the Lesson activity enforces an order on the student. However, you may want to orient your new student before allowing them this freedom.

Administration

Only teachers, course creators, and site administrators can see the Administration block.

It is hidden from students. For that reason, there is very little disadvantage to having this block displayed. It appears on the Front Page and each course's Home Page by default. Consider keeping it unless you have a specific, compelling reason to hide it.

The Administration options apply to the entire site, not just to the Front Page.

When this block appears on the site's Front Page, an Admin link appears at the bottom of the block. Clicking this takes the user to an Administration page with choices that apply to the entire site:

Administration

Configuration

Variables – Configure variables that affect general operation of the site
Site settings – Define how the front page of the site looks
Themes – Choose how the site looks (colors, fonts etc)
Language – For checking and editing the current language pack
Modules – Manage installed modules and their settings
Blocks – Manage installed blocks and their settings
Filters – Choose text filters and related settings
Backup – Configure automated backups and their schedule
Editor settings – Define basic settings for HTML editor

Users

Authentication – You can use internal user accounts or external databases
Edit user accounts – Browse the list of user accounts and edit any of them
Add a new user – To manually create a new user account
Upload users – Import new user accounts from a text file

Enrolments – Choose internal or external ways to control enrolments
Enroll students – Go into a course and add students from the admin menu
Assign teachers – Find a course then use the icon to add teachers
Assign creators – Creators can create new courses and teach in them
Assign admins – Admins can do anything and go anywhere in the site

Courses   Define courses and categories and assign people to them

Logs   Browse logs of all activity on this site

Site files   For publishing general files or uploading external backups

Calendar

Workshops, assignments, quizzes, and events all have dates, so they all appear on the Calendar.

In the screenshot shown, the colored block next to each of the event types indicates how that type is displayed on the Calendar. To turn off the display of that event type, click the event type. The colored block will disappear and the event type will be taken off the Calendar. Global events are events that you add to the Front Page. Course events are events that you add to a course. Group events are events created by a teacher that are open only to the group of which the student is a member. User events are created by the user. They are personal events, viewable only by the user.

The type of people who will have access to the Front Page determines what event types you will want to display on the Calendar. If your Front Page is open to anonymous, unregistered viewers, you must decide if you want to reveal global, course, group, and user events to them. Will these events act as good sales tools, and inspire people to sign up for your site? Or, will revealing some of these event types betray your users' confidence? Usually, showing global and course an event to anonymous users is a good sales tool, without revealing anything confidential about the enrolled users.

Front Page Description

When you view a course, the course Summary block displays the course summary from the course's Settings page. When you view the Front Page, the Front Page description block displays the Site Description from the Site Settings page.

Like all blocks, the Front Page description appears in the left or right column. Research shows that readers notice items placed in the upper right corner of a web page more than those in other positions. If it's important that new visitors see this block, consider placing it there.

Welcome to the *Wilderness Skills* site. If you have an interest in primitive living/survival skills, you're at the right place. This site offers courses in basic botany (just enough for a beginning forager), shelter building, firestarting without matches, orienteering, and other wilderness skills.

The first course, *Basic Botany for Foragers*, is free. It covers the terms and concepts you need to know to understand most field guides and to talk about wild plants. Try the free course, and if you like it, you can join us for other courses for a low fee.

Also, remember that this block is essentially a full-featured web page. The editing window for creating this text is that same one that Moodle gives you for creating web pages. You can use text styles, graphics, even embedded multi-media objects or *JavaScript* in this block. The Front Page description is your first and best chance to convince visitors to go beyond the Front Page. Use it well.

In addition to appearing on the Front Page, the Site Description also appears in the meta tag for your site. The following figure is the source code for the Front Page of the example site. Notice the Site Description appears in the meta tag named "description".

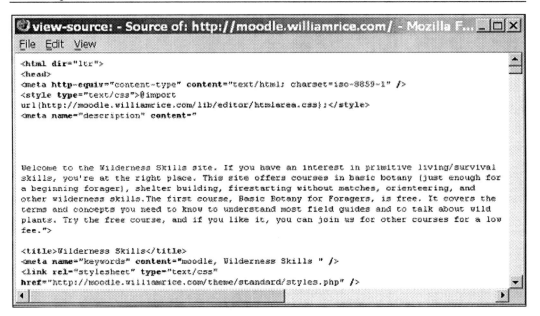

Most search engines use the description meta tag to classify your site. In some cases, the first words in this meta tag appear in search results. When writing the Site Description, write the first few sentences to be search-engine friendly. Imagine that these sentences are what someone will see when your site is displayed in search engine results. Also, don't be afraid to use text styles, graphics, and other web page features in the description.

Courses

The Courses block displays links to the course categories. Clicking a link takes the student to the list of courses. Recall that on the Site Settings page, you can choose to display a list of course categories, or a list of courses. Either of these will appear in the centre of the page.

In the previous figure, I've displayed the Courses block, and also the list of courses using the setting from the Site Settings page. Of course, these lists are redundant. However, this gives you the chance to compare the two methods of listing your courses, side by side. Notice that displaying the courses in the centre of the page makes them much more prominent. If you use the Courses block instead of displaying the course list in the centre of the page, consider including some text on the Front Page that instructs visitors to choose a course category from the Courses block when they are ready to enter a course.

Latest News

By default, the Front Page has a news forum. The Latest news block displays the most recent postings from this forum.

Even if the forum is renamed, this block displays the postings. The number of postings displayed in this block is determined in the Site Settings page, by the field News items to show. On my site, I want to change the title of this block to Latest Site News. To do this, I look in the file /lang/en/moodle.php for $string['latestnews'] = 'Latest News'; and change it to $string['latestnews'] = 'Latest Site News'.

If you have set the news forum to email students with new postings, you can be reasonably sure that the students are getting the news so you might not need to display this block. However, if the news items are of interest to visitors not enrolled in your site, you probably want to display this block so that they will be notified of the news items.

Login

The Login block is available only for the site's Front Page.

After the user logs in, this block disappears. If a visitor is not logged in, Moodle displays small Login links in the upper right corner and bottom centre of the page. However, the links are not very noticeable. The Login block is much more prominent, and contains a message encouraging visitors to sign up for an account.

The main advantage to the Login block over the small Login links is the block's greater visibility. However, if you want to make the Login link in the upper right larger, look in Moodle's index.php file for this line:

```
$loginstring = "<font size=2> <a href=\"$wwwroot/login/index.php\">"
.get_string("login")."</a></font>";
```

Change <font size=2> to a larger number. This increases the font size of the Login link.

If you want to edit the message displayed in the Login block, look for the string startsignup in the the file moodle.php in the language folder. In my example site, I'm using the language en_us, so I look in the file /lang/en_us/moodle.php for this line:

```
$string['startsignup'] = 'Start now by creating a new account!';
```

I can change the message to something else, such as Click here to sign up!.

Main Menu

The Main menu block is available only on the site's Front Page. Anything that can be added to a course can be added to this block, as you can see from the pull-down menus labeled Add a resource and Add an activity.

In my example site, I use the Main menu to convey information about the site and how to use the site. I want visitors to be able to easily get instructions for enrolling and using courses. Perhaps I should change the name of this block to How to Use this Site. I can do that by looking in the language folder for the file moodle.php, for this line:

```
$string['mainmenu'] = 'Main Menu';
```

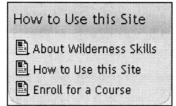

Change Main menu to whatever you want displayed for the name of the menu.

Online Users

The Online Users block shows who is on the site at the present time. Every few minutes, the block checks who is on the site. You set the number of minutes under Administration | Configuration | Blocks | Online Users | Settings.

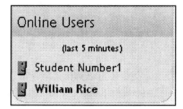

Note that the users can be anywhere on the site; the block does not tell you where. Also note that it tells you who is on the site now; it is not a complete list of everyone who is registered on the site.

When a visitor clicks on a user's name in this block, Moodle displays the user's profile. However, if the variable forceloginforprofiles is set to Yes (under Administration | Configuration | Variables), then the visitor must create an account and log in to see the user's profile.

Remember that Moodle can authenticate users against an external database. For example, if your school or company uses an LDAP database for email accounts, you can authenticate Moodle users against that. Remember also that you can bring data from the LDAP database into the Moodle users' profiles. Before you reveal users' names and profiles to the world, consider whether their Moodle profile contains any information that you might want to keep private.

People

When the People block is added to the site's Front Page, it lists the users enrolled on the site.

When it's added to a course, it lists the users enrolled in that specific course. If the site or course uses groups, it provides a link to those groups. It also provides a link to the user's profile page.

In the Site settings page, you use the showsiteparticipantslist field to determine who can see this list: students and teachers, or just teachers.

Recent Activity

When the Recent activity block is added to the site's Front Page, it lists all of the student and teacher activity on the Front Page since the user's last login.

If someone is logged in as a guest user, this block displays activity since the last time guest logged in. If guest users are constantly coming to your site, this block may be of limited use to them. One strategy is to omit this block from the site's Front Page, so anonymous users don't see it, and add it only to courses that require users to log in.

Search

The Search block provides a search function for forums. It does not search other types of activities or resources. When this block is added to the site's Front Page, it searches only the Forums on the Front Page.

This block is different from the Search courses field that automatically appears on the site's Front Page. The Search courses field searches course names and descriptions for the search terms.

Upcoming Events

The Upcoming Events block is an extension of the Calendar block. It gets event information from your Calendar. By default, the Upcoming Events block displays a maximum of 10 upcoming events. It looks ahead a maximum of 21 days.

These limits are set in the file /blocks/calendar/lib.php, in these lines:

```
define ('CALENDAR_UPCOMING_DAYS', 21);
define ('CALENDAR_UPCOMING_MAXEVENTS', 10);
```

Combining Anonymous, Guest, and Registered Access

There are three ways by which you can gain access into Moodle: Anonymous, Guest, and Registered access. However, you need to know which kind of user access is best for your learning site. Because the different kinds of access can be applied to the site and individual courses, you can combine them to create the effect you want. This will be explained in the following section.

Security Options Available to You

Moodle's security options enable you to choose the kind of user access that is best for your learning site. From the moment that a web browser hits your Moodle site until the student has enrolled in a course, those options are:

- Add your own introductory page, index.html, to the Moodle directory. When browsers first visit your site, instead of seeing Moodle's Front Page they'll see index.html. This enables you to create exactly the first impression you want, without the limitations imposed by Moodle's layout.

- Enable anonymous access or require login to the Front Page. Which option you use depends upon the purpose of the Front Page. If the Front Page sells your site, you will probably want to allow anonymous access. If the Front Page educates registered users on how to use your site, you will probably want to require registration.

- Enable or disable guest access for individual courses. If you want anonymous visitors to be able to sample your courseware easily, create a course category for free courses and put that prominently on the Front Page. Enable guest access without an enrollment key for these sample courses. Then, you can restrict access to your core courses to registered users only.

- Enable or disable enrollment key for individual courses. You pass the enrollment key to your students outside of Moodle. This gives you another way to authenticate students. You can issue the enrollment key one at a time, after you have confirmed a student's identity and/or they have paid for the course. In that case, in the course settings you would select not to allow guest access, and to use the enrollment key. Then, only registered users with the enrollment key could access the course. Another option is to allow guests into the course with the enrollment key. In that case, the students would remain anonymous because they haven't registered, but there would still be some control on who can access the course. For example, suppose you have a course to help emergency workers deal with the stress of their jobs. You might want to give students the option of remaining anonymous, by allowing guest access. However, you don't want the entire world to be able to access the course. So, you could distribute the enrollment key to the users via their agency's email, or a memo in their inboxes, or some other means that ensures that only the intended audience gets the enrollment key.

- Segregate courses into groups. Remember that for each kind of activity, you can turn the group mode on and off. This offers an even finer layer of security than just regulating access to courses. You can allow open access to a course's introductory information, and then turn on group mode for the activities in the course.

Look and Feel

You can brand your learning site with your own colors, fonts, styles, logo, and text messages.

Themes: Customize Colors and Styles

In Moodle, the theme determines the colors and font styles that your site uses. To choose a theme, select Administration | Configuration | Themes. The choices you see there are standard themes that come with Moodle. On your server, you will find the files for these themes in /theme. Compare the theme names available in the Themes page with the directories you see on the server:

Instead of modifying a standard theme, duplicate the theme that is closest to what you want and modify the duplicate. Also, check `http://moodle.org/` for other themes that you can use. For example, the theme called *Kubrick* gives Moodle a look similar to the default installation of the **WordPress** blogging software. With this theme, your site is hardly recognizable as a Moodle site:

The following sections show you how to achieve some of these customizations.

Custom Logo

Not every theme uses a logo. For example, the theme Standard does not, but standardlogo does. The easiest way to include a customized logo in your Moodle site is to copy a theme that uses a logo, and then replace that theme's logo.jpg file with your own.

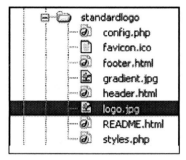

Custom Header and Footer

Inside the Theme folder you will find the files header.html and footer.html. These are displayed as the header and footer on each page. Notice that the Home Page (Front Page) of your site uses a different header than the inside pages. If you want to use the same header on the inside pages and Front Page, you'll need to customize both headers.

Customizing the Header

The lines that you need to customize in header.html are inside the <table> element. The text that you would replace with your customized header is in bold:

```
<table width="100%" cellpadding="0" cellspacing="0" border="0"
class="headerhome">
    <tr>
      <td valign="top" class="headerhomemain">
      <img border="0"src="<?php echo $standardlogo ?>"></td>
      <td align="right" valign="top" class="headerhomemenu">
      <?php echo $menu ?></td>
    </tr>
</table>
    <?php } else if ($heading) {  // This is what gets printed on any
    other page with a heading ?>
<table width="100%" cellpadding="0" cellspacing="0" border="0"
    class="header">
    <tr>
      <td valign="top" class="headermain"><?php echo $heading?></td>
      <td align="right" valign="top" class="headermenu"><?php echo
      $menu ?></td>
    </tr>
</table>
```

The first line, `<img border="0" src="<?php echo $standardlogo ?>">`, inserts your logo into the header. If you want to retain your logo, keep this text. The second line, `<?php echo $menu ?>`, inserts the login and language menus to the right of the logo. Remember that you can choose to hide and show these on the Variables page.

If you want to add a second line to the header, so that the logo and menus appear at the top and your custom content appear below them, add another row to the table. For example, the row in bold was added to the Front Page header table. It adds a line of text with a link below the logo and menu:

```
<table width="100%" cellpadding="0" cellspacing="0" border="0"
class="headerhome">
    <tr>
      <td valign="top" class="headerhomemain"><img
      border="0" src="<?php echo $standardlogo ?>"></td>
      <td align="right" valign="top" class="headerhomemenu"><?php
      echo $menu ?></td>
    </tr>
    <tr>
      <td valign="top" class="headerhomemain"><p><a
      href=http://williamrice.com/wilderness.html>
      Check out</a> our wilderness skills classes given in the
      beautiful, wild
      mountains of West Virginia!</p></td>
      <td align="right" valign="top" class="headerhomemenu"><?php
      echo $menu ?></td>
    </tr>
</table>
```

Customizing the Footer

The `footer.html` file is even simpler and easier to customize than the header. It consists of these lines:

```
<!-- START OF FOOTER -->
<center>
<hr size="1" noshade="noshade" />
<p class="logininfo"><?php echo $loggedinas ?></p>
<p class="homelink"><?php echo $homelink ?></p>
</body>
</html>
```

This inserts a horizontal ruling line, then the "You are logged in as" notice below, and then a Moodle logo that links to `http://www.moodle.org` below. You can edit, delete, or add to this as you wish. However, remember that if you remove the menu from the header `<?php echo $menu ?>` and also remove `<?php echo $loggedinas ?>` from the footer, the user will not see any confirmation that (s)he has logged in. You should keep at least one of these on the page.

Custom Icons

Icons for your Moodle site are in the directory /moodle/pix. Subdirectories inside /pix organize the icons by their purpose:

- /moodle/pix/c holds course icons. For example, it holds the icons that appear before course names, event names, and groups.

- /moodle/pix/f holds mostly icons for the various file formats. For example, it holds icons for text files, videos, and excel files.

- /moodle/pix/g holds the pictures that teachers upload to their personal profiles. The default Moodle installation has two files in this directory: a large and small happy face.

- /moodle/pix/i holds Moodle's navigation and function icons. For example, there are icons for the edit function, to hide and show items, and to show the news.

- /moodle/pix/m holds icons for currency.

- /moodle/pix/s holds icons for smilies: angry, sad, wink, etc.

- /moodle/pix/t holds icons that appear in teacher's functions: backup, delete, hide, and restore.

- /moodle/pix/u holds pictures that students upload to their personal profiles. The default Moodle installation has two files in this directory: a large and small happy face.

You can replace any of these icons with your own. However, if you change the size of an icon, you should preview the results on several pages to ensure the icon still fits in the space that Moodle gives it.

Custom Strings

In this and earlier chapters, you saw that editing strings in the file /lang/en/moodle.php enables you to customize the messages, prompts, and box names that Moodle displays. If you look in the folder /lang/en, you will see many other files in that directory. These files contain strings for Moodle's additional modules. For example, /lang/en/forum.php contains strings for forums, such as $string['deleteddiscussion'] = 'The discussion topic has been deleted.' If you want to customize a string and you're unsure where to find it, use your HTML editor (or even your word processor) to search the files in the language directory for that string.

Summary

First impressions are as important for a learning site as for a job interview. By customizing your site's Front Page, and opening access to sample learning material, you can give potential students the best impression. Customizing your site's logo, header/footer, icons, and strings takes a slightly higher level of technical skills, but results in a site that conveys your unique brand.

Features for Teachers

Moodle keeps detailed logs of all activities that users perform on your site. You can use these logs to determine who has been active in your site, what they did, and when they did it.

Moodle has a modest log viewing system built into it. However, for sophisticated log analysis, you need to look outside Moodle. The following section will help you with the tools you need to view and analyze your site logs.

Logs: Where Are They Stored?

Unlike some programs, Moodle does not store logs as text files. Instead, it stores the logs in the Moodle database. The following screenshot shows the first few lines of my site's log:

	id	time	userid	ip	course	module	cmid	action	url	info
□ ✎ ✗	1	1110902813	1	146.203.50.85	1	user	0	update	view.php?id=1&course=1	
□ ✎ ✗	2	1114089138	0	146.203.50.85	0	login	0	error	http://moodle.williamrice.com/login/index.php	admin
□ ✎ ✗	3	1114089145	0	146.203.50.85	0	login	0	error	http://moodle.williamrice.com/login/index.php	admin
□ ✎ ✗	4	1114089149	1	146.203.50.85	1	user	0	login	view.php?id=1&course=1	1
□ ✎ ✗	5	1114132470	1	24.185.54.44	1	user	0	login	view.php?id=1&course=1	1
□ ✎ ✗	6	1114137884	1	24.185.54.44	1	user	0	logout	view.php?id=1&course=1	1
□ ✎ ✗	7	1114169804	1	146.203.50.85	1	user	0	login	view.php?id=1&course=1	1
□ ✎ ✗	55	1115044485	1	146.203.50.85	6	course	0	new	view.php?id=6	
□ ✎ ✗	9	1114172679	1	146.203.50.85	1	user	0	logout	view.php?id=1&course=1	1
□ ✎ ✗	10	1114172747	0	146.203.50.85	1	library	0	mailer	http://moodle.williamrice.com/login/signup.php	ERROR: The following From address failed: williamr...
□ ✎ ✗	11	1114172778	1	146.203.50.85	1	user	0	login	view.php?id=1&course=1	1

Notice that the time is stored in ascending order. This means that the lines you see at the beginning of the log are the oldest entries.

But when Moodle displays log files, it does so in reverse order; it displays the most recent entries first. You would need to scroll to the end of Moodle's log display to see the oldest entries.

Moodle's Logs Page

Here is a screenshot of the site's log as it appears in Moodle's Logs page:

Notice that Moodle's display of the log files can be filtered by course, participant, day, and activity. When you select Logs from the Admin block on the site's Front Page, the first drop-down list is set to select the entire site. You can change this to select a single course instead. If you select Logs from the Admin block within a course, the log display will be set to that course. Once again, you can always change it.

You cannot select multiple values for any of these variables. That is, you cannot select two courses for the first drop-down list, then four participants from the second, and a few days from the third. If you want a more sophisticated view of the logs, you must use a tool other than Moodle's built-in log viewer. Unfortunately, you cannot just download the logs as text files and import them into a log viewer. Moodle does not offer a direct way to download log files. The next subsection tells you how to download your site logs so that you can use them in a more sophisticated log viewer.

Export Logs using phpMyAdmin

phpMyAdmin is installed by many hosting services. In the Moodle installation chapter, you saw how to use this product to edit the Moodle database directly. You can also use it to export data from the database.

In the following screenshot, the table mdl_log has been selected, which contains log data. Then the Export tab was selected. In this example, because I'm preparing to import the log data into **Microsoft Excel**, under Export, CSV for MS Excel was selected. This same setting will work if you're importing the data into **OpenOffice's** spreadsheet. Also notice that Put fields names at first row has been selected, so that we get the field names in the exported file. To save this as a file on the local hard drive, the Save as file checkbox has been selected:

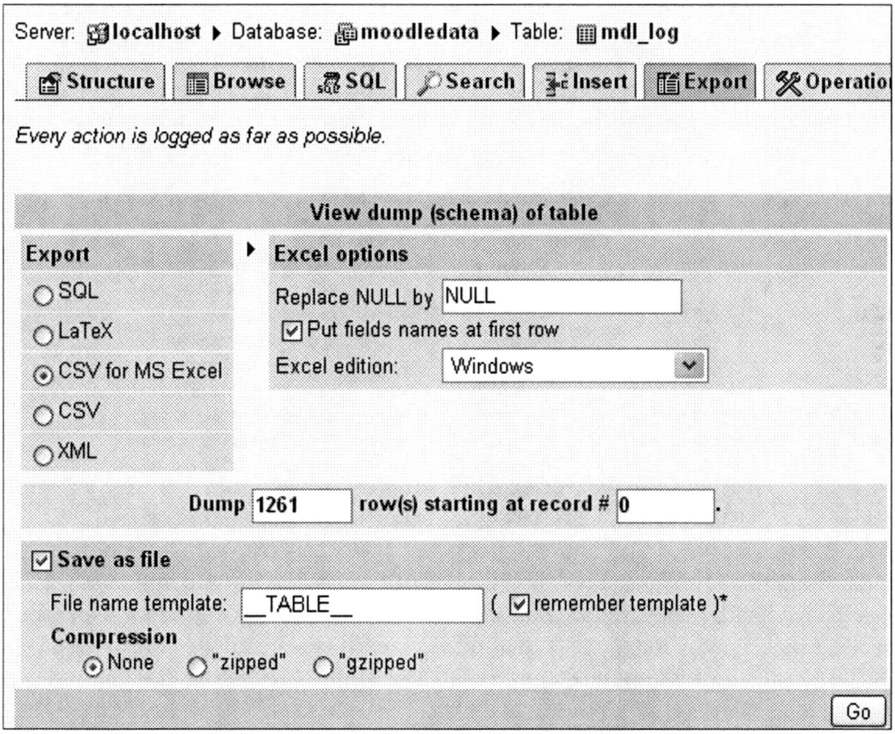

phpMyAdmin saved the file on my local hard drive as `mdl_log.csv`. The next step was to launch Microsoft Excel, and import the file. Because this file was exported specifically for Excel, importing it is as simple as opening it from within Excel:

The following figure is the log file in Excel. Notice these are the same ten lines you saw in Moodle's Logs page, and while browsing the database with phpMyAdmin:

A	B	C	D	E	F	G	H	I	
	time	userid	ip	course	module	cmid	action	url	info
1	1110902813	1	146.203.50.85	1	user	0	update	view.php?id=1&course=1	
2	1114089138	0	146.203.50.85	0	login	0	error	http://moodle.williamrice.com/login/index.php	admin
3	1114089145	0	146.203.50.85	0	login	0	error	http://moodle.williamrice.com/login/index.php	admin
4	1114089149	1	146.203.50.85	1	user	0	login	view.php?id=1&course=1	
5	1114132470	1	24.185.54.44	1	user	0	login	view.php?id=1&course=1	
6	1114137884	1	24.185.54.44	1	user	0	logout	view.php?id=1&course=1	
7	1114169804	1	146.203.50.85	1	user	0	login	view.php?id=1&course=1	
55	1115044485	1	146.203.50.85	6	course	0	new	view.php?id=6	
9	1114172679	1	146.203.50.85	1	user	0	logout	view.php?id=1&course=1	

Notice that the userid field displays the number of the user, not the name. Also notice that the course field displays the course number instead of a user-friendly course name. To find out what these codes mean, you need to look inside the database. Once again, I use phpMyAdmin, and view the mdl_course table. The following screenshot shows course IDs 1 and 5:

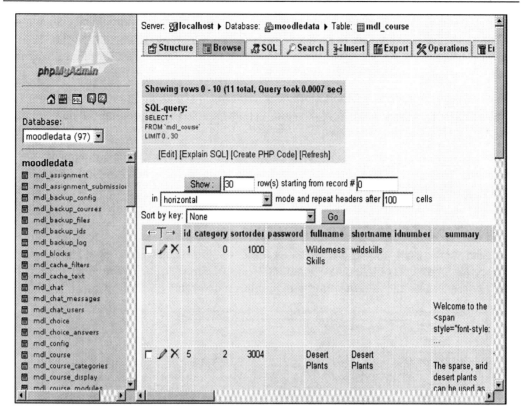

With the data in Excel, you can use Excel's data menu to format, chart, and analyze the data. A complete discussion of Excel's data functions is beyond this book, but there are many sources of help for these functions. The lower figure opposite is an example of a table created in Excel from the imported data. The data cells contain the number of course actions performed by each user in each course. At a glance, you can see which users and courses are most active.

Using Scales for Feedback, Rating, and Grading

In Moodle, you can use scales to rate or grade forums, assignments, quizzes, lessons, journals, and workshops. These scales can be used by anyone who is grading or evaluating a student's work. For example, if a workshop is being graded by other students, then the students use the scale selected by the teacher to grade that workshop. Being able to apply a scale to so many types of activities is a powerful way to make your courses more interactive and engaging.

Moodle comes with two preexisting scales. One is called "Separate and Connected Ways of Knowing". This scale enables students to describe an item as connected to other knowledge in the course, or separate from the other knowledge. It isn't useful as a way to grade students, but instead is used to stimulate discussion about the item.

The other built-in scale that Moodle offers is numeric. You can assign a maximum number of points, from 1 to 100, to an item. Whoever is rating or grading the item selects a numeric grade from a drop-down list.

Moodle also enables you to create custom scales. This is covered in the subsequent subsection. But first, let's see how to apply a scale to an activity, and how to use that scale to grade a student's submission.

Applying a Scale to an Activity

In the next screenshot, I've added a grading scale to a journal activity. I could have selected No Grade, Separate and Connected Ways of Knowing, or any number from 1 to 100. I chose to give this journal entry a maximum point value of 10:

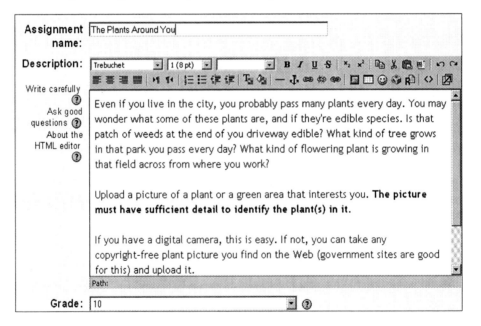

When a teacher views this journal assignment, the teacher clicks the Grade button to display a pop-up window where the teacher can view the uploaded file, write a comment, and select the numeric grade:

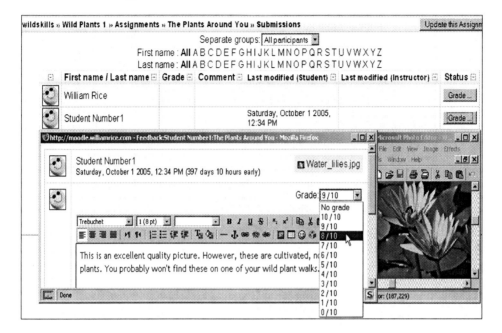

If No Grade were selected for this assignment, only the comments would be available. The drop-down list of grades would not appear.

Establishing Custom Scales

The site administrator can create custom grading scales that are available to all teachers. A teacher can also create a custom scale to be used in the course in which it is created. A custom scale consists of a list of choices that you enter in an ascending order.

For example, you can create a scale for students to rate forum posts that reads: 1-Does not apply to our discussion topic, 2-Partially applies to our discussion topic, 3-Mostly applies to our discussion topic, 4-Totally on target for our discussion topic:

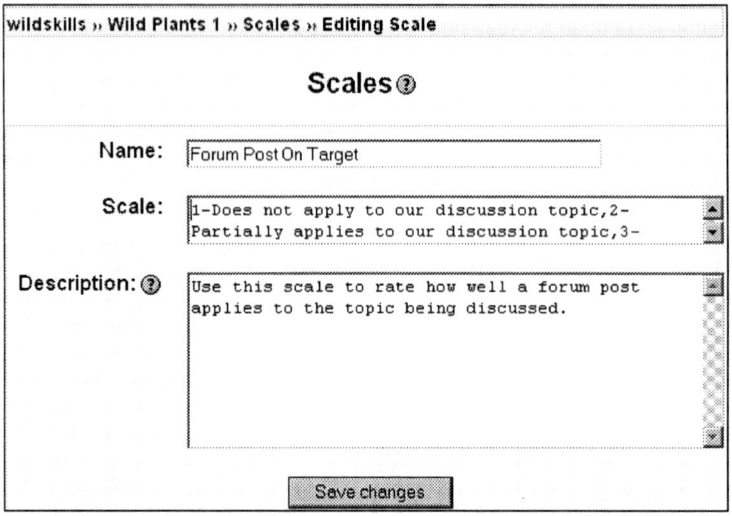

```
wildskills » Wild Plants 1 » Scales » Editing Scale

                        Scales ⓘ

        Name:    Forum Post On Target

        Scale:   1-Does not apply to our discussion topic,2-
                 Partially applies to our discussion topic,3-

  Description: ⓘ  Use this scale to rate how well a forum post
                 applies to the topic being discussed.




                      Save changes
```

To reach the Scales page, select Scales from the Administration block. Then click the Add a new scale button. That will display a window like the one shown in the figure.

Grades

Moodle offers a very flexible reporting tool for grades. When you combine the ability to customize grading scales with Moodle's extensive grading tools, you have a powerful way to view the progress of your students. As a teacher, you can categorize graded activities, assign ranges to letter grades, use weighted grades, and hide/reveal grades to students. If Moodle doesn't have the reporting capabilities you want, you can download grades in text-only or Excel format and use a spreadsheet to chart and analyze them.

Anything that can have a scale applied to it can be graded: forums, assignments, quizzes, lessons, journals, and workshops.

> Remember from the previous section on Scales that grades can be assigned by both teachers and students.

Viewing Grades

To access grades, select the course whose grades you want to see, and then select Grades from the Administration block. This displays a summary of the grades for that course:

Notice that Student 2 has not completed any of the assignments in this course. Student 1 has earned a total of 15.33 points out of a possible 35. We know that all of the grades are Uncategorised because that is the only category with a link. To investigate the grades further, click the Uncategorised link and the detailed grades will display:

Now you can see why Student 1's overall grade is so low. For the assignment *Observing the Familiar*, the student has a grade of zero out of a possible 16 points. We know the student has not completed that assignment because Excluded displays where the percentage would be. If the student has completed the assignment but earned zero points, then 0% would display instead.

Categorizing Grades

Each of the graded activities can be put into a category. Note that you put activities into categories, not students. If you want to categorize students, put them into groups. Categorizing the graded activities in a course enables you to quickly see how your students are doing with various kinds of activities. If you do not assign an activity to a category, by default it belongs to the category Uncategorised.

Creating and Viewing Categories

In the next example, the Set Categories tab has been selected and two categories for activities have also been created:

The result of creating these categories is a more useful view of my students' grades. Here is the View Grades tab now:

Now I can immediately see where Student 1 has the most problem: with student-graded activities.

The most important point here is to determine what kind of question you want to answer when you examine student grades, and create categories that enable you to answer that question. For example, "How do my students do on quizzes versus more interactive activities, like workshops and forums?" To answer that question, create a category just for quizzes, and you can answer that question just by viewing the grades.

Using Extra Credit

You can designate any activity as extra credit under the Set Categories tab. In this example, I'm setting the Course Discussion as extra credit:

Grade Item	Category	Max Grade	Curve To	Extra Credit
Course Discussion	Teacher-graded Activities ▾	1	1	☑
The Plants Around You	Student-graded Activities ▾	10	10	☐
What kind of plant is it?	Teacher-graded Activities ▾	3	3	☐
Leaf Types and Shapes	Teacher-graded Activities ▾	5	5	☐
Observing the Familiar	Student-graded Activities ▾	16	16	☐

View Grades | Set Preferences | Set Categories | Set Weights | Set Grade Letters | Grade Exceptions

Set Categories ⑦

Save Changes

In an earlier screenshot, you saw that the category Teacher-graded Activities had a total of nine points possible. Now that the Course Discussion has been designated as extra credit, this category has a total of eight points possible:

View Grades | Set Preferences | Set Categories | Set Weights | Set Grade Letters | Grade Exceptions

Download in Excel format | Download in text format

All grades by category ⑦

Student Sort by Lastname Sort by Firstname	Student-graded Activities Stats		Teacher-graded Activities Stats		Total Stats		Student Sort by Lastname Sort by Firstname
	points(26)	Percent	points(8)	Percent	points (34) ↓↑	% ↓↑	
Number1, Student	8	30.77%	7.33	91.63%	15.33	45.09%	Number1, Student
Number2, Student	0	0%	-	0%	-	0%	Number2, Student

While it may be tempting to create a category just for extra credit activities, Moodle recommends against making all of the activities in a category extra credit. This might cause errors in the program, and might cause those activities to not even register. Instead, use the extra credit setting on selected activities in a category.

Grading on a Curve

The Set Categories tab gives you the ability to grade any activity on a curve. This means that instead of the activity receiving the total number of points set in the activity's Settings page, it receives the number of points that you enter under the Set Categories tab. In this example, I've assigned the three-question quiz nine points. Each question in the quiz now contributes three points to the total grade:

View Grades	Set Preferences	Set Categories	Set Weights	Set Grade Letters	Grade Exceptions

Set Categories ⑦

Grade Item	Category	Max Grade	Curve To	Extra Credit
Course Discussion	Teacher-graded Activities ▾	1	1	☑
The Plants Around You	Student-graded Activities ▾	10	10	☐
What kind of plant is it?	Teacher-graded Activities ▾	3	9	☐
Leaf Types and Shapes	Teacher-graded Activities ▾	5	5	☐
Observing the Familiar	Student-graded Activities ▾	16	16	☐

Save Changes

Looking under the View Grades tab, you can see that now the total number of points for Teacher-graded Activities has changed from eight to fourteen:

View Grades	Set Preferences	Set Categories	Set Weights	Set Grade Letters	Grade Exceptions

Download in Excel format   Download in text format

All grades by category ⑦

Student Sort by Lastname Sort by Firstname	Student-graded Activities Stats		Teacher-graded Activities Stats		Total Stats		Student Sort by Lastname Sort by Firstname
	points(26)	Percent	points(14)	Percent	points (40) ↓↑	% ↓↑	
Number1, Student	8	30.77%	7.33	52.36%	15.33	38.33%	Number1, Student
Number2, Student	0	0%	-	0%	-	0%	Number2, Student

When to use Curve and When to use Weight

Grading on a curve is a convenient way to compensate for a single activity that proved too easy or too difficult. For example, if all of your students did poorly in a quiz, you could curve the quiz to a lower number of points, or even give it zero points. Your students could still see their quiz grades, but the zero points would eliminate it from their total grade.

Note that given a single activity a zero point value is different than hiding it.

Under the Set Weights tab, you can hide an entire category of activities so that their grades are not displayed to the students, and are not used in the total calculation. A curve affects just a single activity, and still enables students to see their grades.

Use a curve when you want to adjust the amount that a *single activity* contributes to the total. Use weighting (covered in the next subsection) when you want to adjust the amount that an *entire category* contributes to the total.

Compensate for a Difficult or Easy Category by Weighting Grades

The Set Weights tab contains several settings to help you adjust how much a category contributes to the point total. You can use these settings to compensate for an especially difficult or easy category.

Weight

You can assign a weight to a grade category. By default, a weight of 100 is applied to the Uncategorised category. This doesn't mean that none of the other categories count towards the total. It means that each category is outweighed:

Dropping the Lowest Scores in a Category

Weighting is intended to enable you to adjust the scores in an entire category of activities, when those activities have proven too difficult or too easy. One way to do this is giving a category a lower or higher weight than the others. Another way to improve the scores in a difficult category is to use Drop X Lowest to drop the lowest scored activities from that category's grades. Before using this feature, make sure every activity in that category has the same point value. The setting will work when the activities have different values, but the results become meaningless. For example, in the next screenshot you can see that there are three Teacher-graded Activities, each with a different point value. If you use Drop X Lowest to drop the lowest-scored activity from that category, the score for Course Discussion would almost always be dropped because a perfect score of 1 would still be lower than a bad score in What kind of plant is it? or Leaf Types and Shapes.

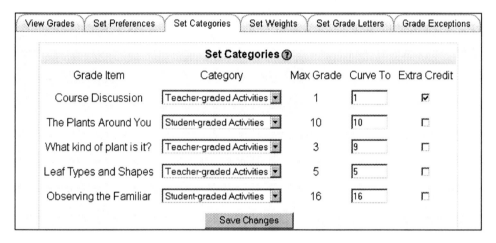

Giving Bonus Points

The Set Weights tab enables you to give all bonus points to every student's total grade in a category. This is a good way to compensate for a category of activities that was too hard. The bonus points show up on the View Grades tab. Note the +2 displayed for the Teacher-graded Activities:

Student	Student-graded Activities Stats		Teacher-graded Activities Stats		Total Stats		Student
Sort by Lastname Sort by Firstname	points(26)	Percent	points(14) (+2)	Percent	points (40) ↓↑	% ↓↑	Sort by Lastname Sort by Firstname
Number1, Student	8	30.77%	9.33	66.64%	17.33	43.33%	Number1, Student
Number2, Student	0	0%	2	14.29%	2	14.29%	Number2, Student

All grades by category ⑦

Hide Ungraded Activities

Under the Set Weights tab, selecting the Hidden checkbox removes a category from display and also from grade calculation. This is an easy way to add items to the grade calculation only after they have been graded. Just keep an activity Uncategorised until you've graded it. After grading, move the activity to the appropriate category. It then becomes visible to the students and is used in the grade totals.

Points, Percents, and Letter Grades

The Set Grade Letters tab enables you to determine the percentages that apply to each letter grade. Moodle comes with suggested values. You can change these at any time, for any course. Note that your change applies only to the course with which you are working:

FREE COURSE: Basic Botany for Foragers   You are logged in as William Rice (Logout)

wildskills » Wild Plants 1 » Grades » **Set Grade Letters**

| View Grades | Set Preferences | Set Categories | Set Weights | Set Grade Letters | Grade Exceptions |

Set Grade Letters ⑦

Grade Letter	Low	High
A	93	100
A-	90	92.99
B+	87	89.99
B	83	86.99
B-	80	82.99
C+	77	79.99
C	73	76.99
C-	70	72.99
D+	67	69.99

To display letter grades to students and teachers under the Set Preferences tab select those who can view the letter grades.

In the same window, select who can view the points and percentage scores. Take special note of the setting for Show Hidden Items. If this is set to Yes, even though a category has been hidden, it will show to the students. You probably want to keep this set to No, since if you're hiding a category the intent is that students will not see it. The setting Letter Grade determines whether letter grades are calculated based on raw percentages or weighted percentages.

For example, you could choose No for Display Weighted Grades, and let students see their true percentages. Then, select Use Percent for Letter Grade, so that students can see what grade they've earned after the weighting is taken into account.

The Teacher Forum

Each course can have a Forum for the teachers in that course. This is especially useful when several teachers collaborate on a course. The link for the Teacher forum appears in the Administration block, so it is not visible to students because that block does not display for students.

If you are the course creator or a teacher in the course, when you enter the Teacher forum you see several links in the upper right corner:

```
wildskills » Wild Plants 1 » Forums » Teacher forum
                                    (?) [                    ] [ Search forums ]

                                    (?) Everyone can choose to be subscribed
                                           Show/edit current subscribers
                                           Unsubscribe from this forum

                        [        Add a new discussion topic        ]
```

The line Everyone can choose to be subscribed means that right now, all teachers in this course can choose to be subscribed to the Forum or not. Subscribers receive email notices when someone posts to the Forum. Clicking on this link forces all teachers of this course to be subscribed to the Forum. It is one of Moodle's quirks that not only can the course creator force all the teachers to be subscribed, but so can any teacher of this course.

The links for Show/edit current subscribers and Unsubscribe from this forum do exactly what they say.

Summary

Whether in a classroom or online, managing a successful course requires two-way communication between the teacher and students. Constantly monitoring a course's logs and grades gives you an early indication that a class may need a midcourse correction. You can use questions, surveys, and chats to discover specific problems and challenges the students are facing. After bringing the course back on track, custom grading scales, extra credit, and curves can help you to equalize the grades. When teaching online, make a habit of often checking the logs and grades.

9

Extending and Administering Moodle

In the previous chapters, you worked with Moodle's standard modules. For example, assignments, forums, glossaries, lessons, quizzes, surveys, and other course features are all made possible by modules. These standard modules are installed with Moodle. You can also install modules that you get from the official http://www.moodle.org/ site, and from other sites.

Add-On Modules

New modules are constantly being developed. To keep abreast of the latest developments, take an occasional look at the Modules and plugins page, on http://www.moodle.org/ where you get most modules. And even if you're not a programmer, contributing feedback and documentation to the modules in progress is a great help in their development.

Getting Modules

The following screenshot shows you the Modules and plugins page for modules from http://download.moodle.org/modules/. The Assignment module is standard, so it is distributed with Moodle, at the moment. The Appointment module is contributed to the Moodle project, so it must be downloaded and installed separately. The status contrib indicates the module is relatively mature. It is not included in the standard distribution because it works only in Moodle version 1.3.5, as you can see from the third column. At the time of writing, Moodle was up to version 1.5. The Book module is under development, so you use it at your own risk if you have version 1.4.3 of Moodle installed. Clicking discussion for any of these modules takes you to the official Moodle forum for that module.

Module	Size	Downloads	Information	Status
Assignment	45KB	Latest 7030 1.5.x 759 1.4.x 3256 1.3.x 836	Assignments allow the teacher to specify a task that requires students to prepare digital content (any format) and submit it by uploading it to the server. (discussion) • Maintainer: *Martin Dougiamas* • Last modified: *Sunday, 2 October 2005, 10:01 AM* (Changelog) (CVS) • Latest version currently requires: *Moodle 1.5 dev (2005031000)*	**standard**
Appointment	8.7KB	1.3.5 6700	This is a simple module that allows appointments to be made for a given week or topic. (discussion) • Maintainer: *Ben Pirt* • Last modified: *Thursday, 12 August 2004, 03:56 PM*	contrib
Book	99.5KB	1.4.3 11163	Makes it easy to create multi-page resources with a book-like format. This module works very well - the only reason it isn't standard yet is that it will be converted to be a Multipage resource type. (discussion) • Maintainer: *Petr Skoda* • Last modified: *Sunday, 28 August 2005, 10:06 AM*	development

Installing Modules

In the following screenshot, you can see the /mod directory in the Moodle installation. Under that directory is a subdirectory for each module:

				FILE MANAGER				
Location: /www/moodle/moodle/mod								
Select	Type	Permission	User	Group	Size	Date	Filename	
[« BACK]							..	
☐	🗀	drwxr-xr-x	williamr	williamr	4096	Sep 09 22:03	assignment	
☐	🗀	drwxr-xr-x	williamr	williamr	4096	Sep 29 22:05	chat	
☐	🗀	drwxr-xr-x	williamr	williamr	4096	Aug 17 22:05	choice	
☐	🗀	drwxr-xr-x	williamr	williamr	4096	Sep 21 22:06	forum	
☐	🗀	drwxr-xr-x	williamr	williamr	4096	Sep 20 22:03	glossary	
☐	🗀	drwxr-xr-x	williamr	williamr	4096	Sep 29 22:05	hotpot	
☐	🗀	drwxr-xr-x	williamr	williamr	4096	Jul 12 22:17	journal	
☐	🗀	drwxr-xr-x	williamr	williamr	4096	Jul 12 22:17	label	
☐	🗀	drwxr-xr-x	williamr	williamr	4096	Sep 29 22:05	lesson	
☐	🗀	drwxr-xr-x	williamr	williamr	4096	Sep 29 22:05	quiz	
☐	🗀	drwxr-xr-x	williamr	williamr	4096	Sep 05 22:05	resource	
☐	🗀	drwxr-xr-x	williamr	williamr	4096	Sep 29 22:05	scorm	
☐	🗀	drwxr-xr-x	williamr	williamr	4096	Jul 12 22:18	survey	
☐	🗀	drwxr-xr-x	williamr	williamr	4096	Aug 10 22:01	wiki	
☐	🗀	drwxr-xr-x	williamr	williamr	4096	Sep 23 22:05	workshop	
☐	[HTML]	-rw-r--r--	williamr	williamr	0	Jan 22 2005	index.html	
☐	📄	-rw-r--r--	williamr	williamr	1178	Feb 12 2004	README.txt	

Installing a new module is a simple process:

1. Download the module from http://www.moodle.org/, or whichever site supplies you with the module.

2. Copy the module files into the /mod directory, so that the module now lives in its own subdirectory.

3. Make sure all students and teachers are logged out of the site.

4. Log in to your site as the administrator, and go to the Admin page.

5. Select Maintenance Mode. While in this mode, only administrators can log in and use the site.

6. Moodle will search for new modules. When it finds one, it displays a message saying that it is building new module tables. At this point, it is adding tables to the database to accommodate the data that the new module will generate.

7. Click the Continue button to return to the Administration page.

8. Select the link to disable Maintenance Mode.

9. Select the link for Modules. You will see a list of installed modules. The one that you installed should be on that list.

Managing Modules

The main tasks for managing modules are hiding/showing them, changing their settings, and deleting them. All of these tasks are accomplished from the Administration | Configuration | Modules page:

Activity module	Activities	Version	Hide/Show	Delete	Settings
Assignment	1	2005060100	👁	Delete	Settings
Chat	2	2005031000	👁	Delete	Settings
Choice	1	2005041500	👁	Delete	
Forum	17	2005042600			Settings
Glossary	0	2005041900	👁	Delete	Settings
Hot Potatoes Quiz	0	2005031419	👁	Delete	
Journal	1	2005041100	👁	Delete	
Label	5	2004111200	👁	Delete	
Lesson	1	2005060900	👁	Delete	
Questionnaire	0	2005062701	👁	Delete	
Quiz	2	2005060301	👁	Delete	Settings
Resource	11	2005041100	👁	Delete	Settings
SCORM	0	2005052300	👁	Delete	Settings
Survey	7	2005031600	👁	Delete	
Wiki	1	2005031000	👁	Delete	
Workshop	1	2005041200	👁	Delete	

wildskills » Administration » Configuration » Modules

Modules

An open eye icon indicates the module is available. A closed eye icon indicates the module is installed but hidden, so course creators cannot use that module or activities created with it. Click the eye icon to open and close it.

Clicking Delete will delete the module's settings, and everything created with the module, from your site's database. However, it will not delete the module code from the /mod directory. If you do not delete the module's directory from /mod, the next time you access the Administration page, the module will reinstall itself.

Notice that not every module has a Settings link. If a module does have settings, then what you choose on that page will affect all activities created with the module.

You might need to determine if you have the latest version of the module installed. To do this, download the latest version from http://www.moodle.org/ or wherever you obtain the module. Usually, the module will be in a ZIP archive. Unzip the readme.txt file, and look for the version number at the top of that file. Compare it to the version you have installed to determine if you're using the latest.

Creative Usage of Backup and Restore

Moodle enables you to back up and restore the entire site, an individual course, and components within a course. The obvious use for this is disaster recovery. However, you can also make more creative use of this capability. For example, you can:

- Back up a course, and then restore it as a new course, thus creating an exact duplicate
- Back up a component of one course, and then restore that component to a different course
- Back up your entire site, and then restore it to your local PC or another web server, and use the backup as a development environment

This section covers backing up and restoring the entire site, individual courses, and the components within a course.

What Gets Backed Up?

When Moodle creates a backup of your site, it backs up each course individually. The only difference between a site-wide and course backup is that the site-wide backup automatically includes every course, saving you the time of backing up each course one at a time. The following screenshot shows the result of a site-wide backup:

Remote Site	Modified	Size
moodle/		
lib	9/30/2005 5:20 PM	
moodle	9/30/2005 5:03 PM	
moodledata	10/20/2005 4:43 PM	
1	10/19/2005 6:51 PM	
4	10/1/2005 5:25 PM	
cache	10/20/2005 3:35 PM	
sessions	10/21/2005 2:53 PM	
temp	10/20/2005 4:43 PM	
users	9/30/2005 5:23 PM	
backup-bow_drill-20051020-1143.zip	10/20/2005 4:43 PM	3KB
backup-debris_huts-20051020-1143.zip	10/20/2005 4:43 PM	3KB
backup-deer-20051020-1143.zip	10/20/2005 4:43 PM	3KB
backup-desert_plants-20051020-1143.zip	10/20/2005 4:43 PM	2KB
backup-discussion-20051020-1143.zip	10/20/2005 4:43 PM	3KB
backup-freepics-20051020-1143.zip	10/20/2005 4:43 PM	4KB
backup-on_the_beach-20051020-1143.zip	10/20/2005 4:43 PM	3KB
backup-tracking_basics-20051020-1143.zip	10/20/2005 4:43 PM	3KB
backup-water_s_edge-20051020-1143.zip	10/20/2005 4:43 PM	3KB
backup-wild_plants_1-20051020-1143.zip	10/20/2005 4:43 PM	12KB
backup-wildskills-20051020-1143.zip	10/20/2005 4:43 PM	7KB

Notice that the name of each backup file includes the name of the course and the date/time of the backup. The last file backup-wildskills-20051020-1143.zip is the Front Page of the site. This is another example of how the Front Page of your site is essentially just another course.

Each of these .zip files contains an .xml file. The .xml file includes all of the information in the course: all of the web pages, forums and their entries, assignments, etc. It also contains the graphics and uploaded files that are part of the course. Where are those graphics and uploaded files stored? Take a look at the following screenshot:

Remote Site	Modified	Size
⊟ 📁 moodle/		
⊞ 📁 lib	9/30/2005 5:20 PM	
⊞ 📁 moodle	9/30/2005 5:03 PM	
⊟ 📁 moodledata	10/20/2005 4:43 PM	
📁 1	10/19/2005 6:51 PM	
⊟ 📁 4	10/1/2005 5:25 PM	
⊟ 📁 moddata	10/3/2005 2:24 PM	
⊟ 📁 assignment	10/1/2005 5:25 PM	
⊟ 📁 1	10/1/2005 5:33 PM	
📁 1	10/1/2005 5:25 PM	
⊟ 📁 5	10/1/2005 5:34 PM	
🖼 Water_lilies.jpg	10/1/2005 5:34 PM	82KB
⊞ 📁 forum	10/3/2005 2:24 PM	
⊞ 📁 cache	10/20/2005 3:35 PM	
⊞ 📁 sessions	10/21/2005 2:53 PM	
⊞ 📁 temp	10/20/2005 4:43 PM	
⊞ 📁 users	9/30/2005 5:23 PM	
📄 backup-bow_drill-20051020-1143.zip	10/20/2005 4:43 PM	3KB
📄 backup-debris_huts-20051020-1143.zip	10/20/2005 4:43 PM	3KB
📄 backup-deer-20051020-1143.zip	10/20/2005 4:43 PM	3KB
📄 backup-desert_plants-20051020-1143.zip	10/20/2005 4:43 PM	2KB
📄 backup-discussion-20051020-1143.zip	10/20/2005 4:43 PM	3KB
📄 backup-freepics-20051020-1143.zip	10/20/2005 4:43 PM	4KB
📄 backup-on_the_beach-20051020-1143.zip	10/20/2005 4:43 PM	3KB
📄 backup-tracking_basics-20051020-1143.zip	10/20/2005 4:43 PM	3KB
📄 backup-water_s_edge-20051020-1143.zip	10/20/2005 4:43 PM	3KB
📄 backup-wild_plants_1-20051020-1143.zip	10/20/2005 4:43 PM	12KB
📄 backup-wildskills-20051020-1143.zip	10/20/2005 4:43 PM	7KB

As you can see, graphics are stored in the moodledata directory, which is specified in the file config.php by the variable $CFG->dataroot = '/home/williamr/www/moodle/moodledata';. For course number 4, the files are in a folder called moodledata/4.

Moodle Backup versus Database Backup versus Directory Backup

From the previous screenshot, you can see that the Moodle backup, whether it's site-wide or for a single course, creates a ZIP file for each of your course(s). If you needed to restore your entire site, you would have to reinstall the Moodle software and then restore each course, one at a time.

If you back up the entire Moodle database, your backup will include everything in the Moodle backup files plus site settings. However, it will not include graphics and files that students submitted, which are stored in the Moodle data directory. If you needed to restore your entire site, you would have to reinstall the Moodle software, import the database, and then restore the Moodle data directory.

If you back up all of the software directories on your Moodle server, and the Moodle data directory, plus the Moodle database, you are taking a complete snapshot of your entire site. For disaster recovery, this is the best option. This is not something that you can do with Moodle. You must work with your system administrator or host to accomplish this.

Automated Backups of Your Site

You do not manually back up your entire Moodle site on demand. Instead, you use the Administration | Configuration | Backup page to determine when your site gets backed up, what features are backed up, and where the backup files are put. Site-wide backups are automated. However, a single course or part of a course can be backed up upon demand.

The following screenshot shows the backup settings for my demo site:

Backup

Configure automated backups and their schedule

Settings

Include Modules:	No ▾ with user data ▾	Choose whether you want to include course modules, with or without user data, in automated backups
Metacourse:	Yes ▾	If enabled, then metacourse info (inherited enrollments) will be included in automated backups
Users:	Course ▾	Select whether you want to include all the users in the server or only the needed users for each course
Logs:	Yes ▾	If enabled, then course logs will be included in automated backups
User Files:	No ▾	Choose whether user files (eg profile images) should be included in automated backups
Course files:	No ▾	If enabled then course files will be included in automated backups
Messages:	No ▾	If enabled, then instant messages will be included in SITE automated backups
Keep:	1 ▾ Files	How many recent backups for each course do you want to keep? (older ones will be deleted automatically)

Schedule

Active: Yes ▾

Sunday	Monday	Tuesday	Wednesday	Thursday	Friday	Saturday
☑	☑	☑	☑	☑	☑	☑

Execute at: 11 ▾ 35 ▾

Save to: /home/williamr/www/moodle/moodledata ⑦
Full path to the directory where you want to save the backup files
(leave blank to save in its course default dir)

The option for User Files specifies whether to back up the directory /moodledata/users. For this version of Moodle, the only user files stored in that directory are the pictures of themselves that users have uploaded. This directory does not store assignment and workshop files that users have uploaded.

Choosing a Backup Location

Notice the directory name at the bottom of the screen. It specifies the location of the backup files on the server. Moodle is designed to back up the files on the same server which hosts the software.

However, if you're using a UNIX or Linux server, you can work with your system administrator to place the files almost anywhere, even on a different computer. ***nix** operating systems enable you to create aliases for other directories and devices. These aliases are called **symlinks**. If you've been given your own user directory on the Moodle server, or some other machine, you can ask your system administrator to create a symlink to your directory. Then, you specify the symlink as the backup location.

Backing Up the Database

To back up the Moodle database, you can use SQL database commands or a tool like phpMyAdmin, which many hosting services supply. If your site is hosted by your institution, you can work with your system administrator to establish an automated backup routine.

Using phpMyAdmin to Back up the Database

phpMyAdmin is one of the most popular database managers installed on commercial hosting services. Like Moodle, it is written in the PHP programming language, is open-source software, and is freely available. If your institution is hosting Moodle, it also has the capacity to host phpMyAdmin. Consider asking your institution to install it so that you can directly manipulate the Moodle database.

Backing up the Moodle database consists of exporting all of the data to a single file. To do this in phpMyAdmin, select the database and then select the Export function:

In this example, because the entire database is being backed up, Select all has been chosen. This selects all of the tables in the database.

For a file format, SQL is selected. If the site crashes, reinstall all the software and import this file into a MySQL database. Because the ultimate destination of this file is a SQL database, a format that matches has been selected.

The options in the right column will probably have no effect on your export and import (backup and restore). In other situations, they might be relevant, but when you are planning on using the export to fill an empty database with the same structure as the original, those options can be skipped.

Selecting Save as file results in the export being downloaded to your local computer:

Here are some sample lines from my database export:

```
-- --------------------------------------------------------

--
-- Table structure for table `mdl_choice_options`
--

CREATE TABLE `mdl_choice_options` (
   `id` int(10) unsigned NOT NULL auto_increment,
   `choiceid` int(10) unsigned NOT NULL default '0',
   `text` text,
   `maxanswers` int(10) unsigned default '0',
   `timemodified` int(10) NOT NULL default '0',
   PRIMARY KEY  (`id`),
   UNIQUE KEY `id` (`id`),
   KEY `choiceid` (`choiceid`)
) TYPE=MyISAM AUTO_INCREMENT=4 ;

--
-- Dumping data for table `mdl_choice_options`
--

INSERT INTO `mdl_choice_options` VALUES (1, 1, 'Yes, I''ve tried
edible plants found in the wild.', 0, 1120577795);
INSERT INTO `mdl_choice_options` VALUES (2, 1, 'No, not yet.', 0,
1120577795);
INSERT INTO `mdl_choice_options` VALUES (3, 1, 'Sort of. They were
plants that you can find in the wild, but I bought them from a
store.', 0, 1120577795);
```

Notice that the export file contains SQL commands such as CREATE and INSERT. These are the commands that create the database tables and fill them with data. If you ever need to import this data, use phpMyAdmin's SQL tab:

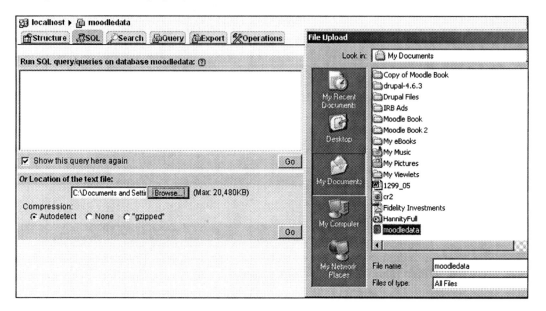

The export file already contains all the SQL commands, so you don't need to enter any into the query area. Instead, just browse, select the file, and then click the Go button. Note that during a normal Moodle installation, the Moodle software creates the database tables. If you restore your database using this method, it is the SQL file, not the Moodle software, that creates the tables.

Backing Up the Moodle Directories

While installing Moodle, we created a directory for the application and a directory for data files. Backing up these directories is as simple as copying them to another computer. In the following screenshot, I'm using DreamWeaver to download these directories from my hosting service to my local computer:

Create a Disaster Recovery Plan

As I mentioned earlier in this chapter, if you back up all of the software directories on your Moodle server, and the Moodle data directory, plus the Moodle database, you are taking a complete snapshot of your entire site. For disaster recovery, this is the best option.

Set Moodle to automatically back up the entire site to the data directory overnight. Keep a week's worth of backups. This is not for disaster recovery, but to give you an easy way to restore any course to the condition it was in a few days ago.

Work with your system administrator to set up automated backup routines that will periodically copy the Moodle application directory, data directory, and export of the database to a different server or your local computer.

Create Different Versions of a Course

At this time, Moodle does not support automatically creating different versions of a course. You can work around this limitation using the following process:

1. Add a new course. You will still need to fill out the Course Settings window and assign a teacher, just as if you were creating a normal course.

2. Once inside the new course, from the Administration panel, select Import Course Data.

3. Moodle displays a window that enables you to select the course that you want to use as a template for this new one. You can search for and select any course in the system. Select the old course, and then click Use this course.

4. The next window displays all of the content types in the course. Select and deselect the appropriate content types, and click the Continue button. If you choose to import the course files, you will also bring in any files that were uploaded to the course by the teacher or course creator. You will not bring in any student files.

5. Select Continue. When the import is complete, you're taken to your new course.

6. Modify the new course as appropriate.

7. Consider putting old courses into a category like "Closed Courses" and closing that category to students. This makes it easier to ensure that you don't accidentally leave an old course open. Or, you can create a subcategory under each category called "Closed Courses", and move old courses there.

Summary

Expanding your Moodle site with additional modules is a powerful tool for customizing and differentiating your e-learning site. Don't be afraid to add modules beyond those that come with the standard Moodle installation package. For example, the Side Bar Block enables you to create activities and resources outside of the middle section, placing them in a sidebar instead of the main course area. If you're worried about the stability or compatibility of add-on modules, you can easily install another Moodle instance just for testing new modules. Work with your system administrator to establish a backup and recovery routine. Add-on modules, Moodle upgrades, and upgrades that your web hosting service make to their software can all bring down your site and/or corrupt your data. A complete software and data backup is a smart investment.

A
The Checklist

This is a basic checklist of tasks for creating an online learning experience with Moodle:

1. Traditional course planning.
   a. Establish your learning objectives. What are the skill- or knowledge-based outcomes you want for this course?
   b. Gather your course material. Moodle can be used to create and support blended learning experiences, so include both online and offline resources.
   c. Evaluate Moodle's "social constructionist" philosophy. Plan the students' learning experience around exploration and interaction.
2. Install and configure Moodle.
   a. If you're installing...
      i. Obtain rights on a web server that has the capabilities needed to run Moodle.
      ii. Create the subdomains and/or directories needed for Moodle and its data.
      iii. Get and unpack Moodle, and upload it to your web server.
      iv. Create the Data directory.
      v. Create the Moodle database.
      vi. Set up the cron job.
      vii. Activate the installation.
   b. If you're administrating the site or creating courses...
      i. Configure site-wide variables.
      ii. Configure site-wide settings.
      iii. Configure authentication and backup options.

3. Create the framework for your learning site.

    a. Create and organize course categories.

    b. Create courses.

        i. Configure course settings.

        ii. Organize courses into categories.

        iii. Assign teachers.

    c. Display site-wide blocks.

    d. Display blocks in specific courses.

4. Add basic course material to your course(s)

    a. Add reading material: text pages and web pages.

    b. Add links to other sites.

    c. Create file directories and add upload files.

    d. Organize material into topics or weeks.

    e. Add labels.

    f. If desired, add the Activities block.

5. Make your courses interactive.

    a. Add assignments.

    b. Add choices (surveys).

    c. Add student journals.

    d. Create lessons.

        i. Design the flow of the lesson.

        ii. Decide grading criteria.

        iii. Add lesson material.

        iv. Add questions and jumps.

    e. Create quizzes.

        i. Create question categories.

        ii. Create questions.

        iii. Arrange questions into quizzes.

6. Make your course social.
    a. Add chat rooms, possibly hiding them until chat time.
    b. If chats are scheduled, show Upcoming Events and Calendar blocks.
    c. Add student forums to site and courses.
    d. Add teacher forums.
    e. Add hidden forums for sending mass emails.
    f. Add local and global glossaries.
    g. Add Wikis and configure for access.
    h. Add workshops.
        i. What will you have each student do?
        ii. Who will assess the assignment(s)?
        iii. How will the assignment(s) be assessed?
        iv. When will students be allowed to submit their assignments?

7. Create a welcome for new and existing students.
    a. Decide whether to allow guest/anonymous access to all or part of site.
    b. Decide whether to show the Login Page or Front Page to new visitors.
    c. Customize the Login Page.
    d. Add material to the Front Page; create a front page "course."
    e. Customize Moodle styles.

8. Use teacher's tools to deliver and administer courses.
    a. Establish custom grading and evaluation scales.
    b. Create teacher forums.
    c. Interpret access logs.
    d. View and download student grades.

9. Extend Moodle with additional modules.
    a. Install and integrate add-on modules.
    b. Test add-on modules.
    c. Back up courses and/or site.
    d. Implement the PayPal module for paid courses or sites.

Index

Thank you for buying Moodle: E-Learning Course Development

Packt Open Source Project Royalties

When we sell a book written on an Open Source project, we pay a royalty directly to that project. Therefore by purchasing *Moodle: E-Learning Course Development*, Packt will have given some of the money received to the Moodle project.

In the long term, we see ourselves and you—customers and readers of our books—as part of the Open Source ecosystem, providing sustainable revenue for the projects we publish on. Our aim at Packt is to establish publishing royalties as an essential part of the service and support a business model that sustains Open Source.

If you're working with an Open Source project that you would like us to publish on, and subsequently pay royalties to, please get in touch with us.

Writing for Packt

We welcome all inquiries from people who are interested in authoring. Book proposals should be sent to authors@packtpub.com. If your book idea is still at an early stage and you would like to discuss it first before writing a formal book proposal, contact us; one of our commissioning editors will get in touch with you.

We're not just looking for published authors; if you have strong technical skills but no writing experience, our experienced editors can help you develop a writing career, or simply get some additional reward for your expertise.

About Packt Publishing

Packt, pronounced 'packed', published its first book "*Mastering phpMyAdmin for Effective MySQL Management*" in April 2004 and subsequently continued to specialize in publishing highly focused books on specific technologies and solutions.

Our books and publications share the experiences of your fellow IT professionals in adapting and customizing today's systems, applications, and frameworks. Our solution-based books give you the knowledge and power to customize the software and technologies you're using to get the job done. Packt books are more specific and less general than the IT books you have seen in the past. Our unique business model allows us to bring you more focused information, giving you more of what you need to know, and less of what you don't.

Packt is a modern, yet unique publishing company, which focuses on producing quality, cutting-edge books for communities of developers, administrators, and newbies alike. For more information, please visit our website: www.PacktPub.com.

Building Websites with Joomla!

ISBN: 1904811949   Paperback: 340 pages

A step-by-step tutorial to getting your Joomla! CMS website up fast

1. Walk through each step in a friendly and accessible way

2. Customize and extend your Joomla! site

3. Get your Joomla! website up fast

Building Online Stores with osCommerce: Professional Edition

ISBN: 1904811140   Paperback: 380 pages

Learn how to design, build, and profit from a sophisticated online business.

1. Install, configure, and customize osCommerce

2. Enhance and modify osCommerce

3. Learn from a sample, fully functional site packed with useful features such as gift certificates and discounts, cross- and up-selling, RSS feed aggregation, enhanced product image handling, and bug fixes.

Please check **www.PacktPub.com** for information on our titles

Printed in the United Kingdom
by Lightning Source UK Ltd.
125955UK00001B/249/A